UP YOUR CASH FLOW™

An Easy-to-Use Business Guide to Immediately Increase Your Profits and Cash Flow

HARVEY A. GOLDSTEIN, CPA

GRANVILLE PUBLICATIONS

ATTENTION:

The author, Harvey A. Goldstein, is available to speak or present seminars on the methods used in *Up Your Cash Flow*. For additional information, contact the publisher at (213) 477-3924 or (213) 879-3501.

ISBN 0-931349-04-4*
ISBN 0-931349-02-8 (Self-Teaching Manual)
Library of Congress Catalog Card Number 84-82281
Including Index

*Formerly "122 Minutes a Month to Greater Profits"

Dedication

To Rochelle, Caryn and Todd,
whom I love.

Table of Contents

About the Author

HARVEY A. GOLDSTEIN is a Certified Public Accountant and managing partner of the Southern California CPA firm of Singer, Lewak, Greenbaum & Goldstein. He has been actively engaged in the practice of public accounting for more than 18 years.

Because of his unparalleled commitment to the small business community, Mr. Goldstein was appointed to President Reagan's National Productivity Advisory Committee, and Mr. Goldstein has been appointed by California Governor George Deukmejian to serve on California's Small Business Development Board.

Mr. Goldstein appears regularly as a guest specialist on local and national radio and television, offering business advice, legislative updates, and tax tips. He speaks to over 100 business groups annually as well as publishing several articles every year. Mr. Goldstein has also authored legislation (The Small Business Investment Incentive Act) designed to stimulate individual investment in American small business.

It is this dedication that has led prestigious publications like *The Wall Street Journal*, *The Washington Post*, the *Los Angeles Times* and *Forbes Magazine* to select Mr. Goldstein to be the subject of several articles. He has been labeled "a crusader for small business," "a man possessed," and "America's small business ally."

Mr. Goldstein's philosophy of business (and life) is best exemplified by a small plaque adorning a corner of his desk in his West Los Angeles office. It reads, "Good Things Come to Those Who Wait— But Only Those Things Left By Those Who Hustle."

Acknowledgements

The ideas in this book are a result of the experiences I have had during many years in public accounting practice. I would like to acknowledge the many clients I have counseled over the years. I have learned everything I know about the techniques and strategies in this book from them.

Many people have assisted me in the preparation of this book. I am very grateful to the following for giving me their comments and counsel: Honay Adams, Bernard Berman, Sheldon Brucker, Jerry Cornwell, Jerry Gross, Paul Gillette, David Krajanowski, Bernard Lewak, Shelly Lowenkopf, Barry Richman, Bob Shmaeff, and Doreen Ward.

Thanks to Joe Kessler for convincing me to write this book and Marty and Sheila McLaughlin for assisting me in its preparation.

A special thanks to Vicki Kohles whose ideas and creativity have touched many pages of this book.

Thank you all.

Preface

A S THE MANAGING PARTNER of an accounting firm, I have been advising small businesses for over 18 years. I have seen many small companies fail and others succeed.

It is obvious that there are two major reasons for the failure of small businesses: poor company management and the lack of sufficient capital.

I believe, as one who has spent so many years in the field of small business, that it is incumbent upon me to share the experiences I have had and to lend my expertise to help solve these problems.

I have attempted to do this in two ways. First, I have written this book which addresses the problems of company management. The book consists of techniques and strategies that will greatly enhance the management capabilities of owners and managers of small and medium-sized companies.

These techniques will result in greater productivity, the ability to understand the results of your company's activity and increase your company's profits. All it will take is 122 minutes a month of your time.

Second, I have attempted to secure legislation which directly addresses the plight of the small business person's inability to raise capital. Chapter 12 of this book discusses the activities I have been pursuing in this area.

By writing this book and working toward the passage of the legislation discussed, I hope I will have contributed in some way toward the success of your business and have helped to strengthen the small business community which is so vital to our country.

1
Whose Business Is It Anyway?

ERNIE HOUSEMAN, Tom Winters, and I were having a meeting to discuss Ernie's frustrations as CEO of their company. "We've got serious problems, and I don't know what to do," Ernie began.

Their company had been undergoing rapid growth, the cash flow was substantial, and Ernie and Tom were comfortably affluent. Ernie's complaint had sounded so familiar. I nodded for him to continue.

"The employees," he said. "They're driving us nuts. Tom and I have been partners for ten years. I'm President, he's Vice President, and we're trapped by details."

Ernie popped out of his chair and began to shout. "We're making $100,000 a piece and we don't know what the hell our functions are. He's off teaching managers how to sell products and I'm solving every damn problem that comes along. We're expanding rapidly but we're losing control. The larger we get, the less either of us knows what's going on, and there are some days when I'm so swamped by details that I don't have time to go to the john."

By now, Ernie was standing in front of me, hands on hips and glaring. Tom was nodding his head in silent, pained agreement with Ernie's outpouring.

Peering over the top of my glasses I said, "I assume you are waiting for me to say something. Well, here it is. I want to find out how each of you spends your time. For the next two weeks, I want each of you to write down everything you do, from the minute you get in to the moment you leave. Be as specific as you can. We'll meet in two weeks and review your lists. From the symptoms, I'd say you can count on some surprises."

Two weeks later, when we met again and the partners handed me their detailed lists of activities, my suspicions were confirmed. I told them, "You are paying an unnecessary $140,000 a year for clerical and secretarial services."

Ernie and Tom looked somber as I explained. Seventy percent of the work performed by each of them—at their own admission—was really the work of an executive secretary or clerk. The partners were splitting $200,000 a year, and the work they performed could have been handled by a $20,000-a-year assistant. Ernie and Tom had become company clerks.

BEING BUSY REDUCES GUILT

Ernie and Tom's dilemma is not unusual. The owner-managers of many small companies often become the company clerk. This happens because there is a level of security achieved when the owner-manager is "busy." Being "busy" tends to satisfy our need to work.

We are all schooled in the concept if we are not pushing, pulling, preparing or being involved in some paperwork, we are not working. To prevent the guilt created by not working we tend to attract lots and lots of details. Eventually every problem within the company must cross our desk—we have become the company clerk.

The basic function of the owner-manager of a small company is difficult to understand. Usually, most owners are highly skilled in a particular field. They tend to work for a company in a specialized area, watch incompetent bosses prosper and then decide "Hell, I can do better than that." They leave the company and they're out on their own.

We've seen it countless times with the machinist who starts a machine shop, the pharmacist who opens a drug store, the computer programmer who opens a consulting business, the carpenter who becomes a contractor, and the garment salesman who becomes a manufacturer. Some of these entrepreneurs become successful but the majority do not. According to recent statistics almost 70 percent of small businesses do not last more than five years.

The managerial skill of the owners and managers is the most important factor in the success or failure of a business. When people go into business, they have a good knowledge of the product or service they provide but little knowledge of managing people, marketing, finance, accounting, inventory controls, and a host of other areas needed to make proper business decisions. Least of all they have little knowledge of the proper function they must perform within their organization.

Ernie and Tom were good examples of this. They were making good money, but they were crying for help. Their frustration with the details of their business became a nightmarish burden. They found themselves wanting to know what to do before it was too late to do anything.

LEADERSHIP—THE CHARACTERISTICS

The owner-manager of a small company is the company's leader. To most owner-managers, leadership is an abstract concept, one not easy to understand.

We've all heard people refer to someone as a good leader. But when asked to explain what that means, it usually boils down to "They seem to get the job done." Rarely do we hear that one is a good leader because he or she has worked at the job well. It's always because they get the job done. In my experience, effective leaders have these traits:

Good Leaders Like What They Do: Is it possible to be successful if you don't like what you do? I've seen it happen, but the general rule is that the love of what one does breeds the greatest success.

Good Leaders Have a Desire for Wealth: Wealth may not be the strongest motivation for success, but it sure does help. Many successful leaders find the love of what they do more of a motivating factor than the promise of wealth. The ideal situation is obviously loving what you do and making money at it.

Good Leaders Are Curious: They always look for better ways to do things. They are curious about the future.

Good Leaders Have Courage: They have the courage to take reasonable risks.

Good Leaders Are Persistent: They tirelessly try to improve their business and themselves. They want to be the best at what they do. They persevere in their desire to solve problems. They rarely give up.

Good Leaders Have the Ability to Motivate: They motivate employees to be more productive, bankers to lend more money, and customers to return. Effective leaders are focused on people and human values.

Good Leaders Have a Strong Ego: Ego satisfaction can be the strongest motivation for success. Many of the most successful business people are driven by powerful egos.

WE ARE THE RULE, NOT THE EXCEPTION

How many of the seven characteristics do you possess? Can you be a successful leader if you only have two or three of the traits mentioned? What if you don't have any? What if you're lucky enough to have all seven, does that guarantee success?

There are more than fifteen million active businesses existing in the U.S. today. If each owner-manager possessed all the qualities outlined for successful leadership, we would indeed be a fortunate nation. We would be a nation with a cadre of highly effective leadership. Unfortunately, we're not.

Writing in *U.S. News and World Report*, Warren Bennis, a Professor of Management at the University of Southern California, indicates effective leadership is the exception, not the rule. He indicates that it is possible to increase the number of people with leadership qualities, but they will always be the exception to the rule. He said, "Individuals need some flair and talent to begin with, but we can help them improve."

Some of us may have the innate flair and talent of good leadership but most of us do not. We are people who have somehow become owners of small companies. Our profits will not be huge and we won't be the subject of magazine articles. Our view of our company will not be based on some grandiose social purpose to aid mankind and we will never think of ourselves as leaders within the community. We will fight and struggle to maintain our capital. We will curse the government every time our taxes are raised and suffer the pain of a jumping prime rate.

THE SEARCH

One day we will look around us, shake our heads, and reflect. "Times have changed." "Employees are different. They don't seem to want to work as hard as we did." "They tell us inflation is down yet expenses are up." "Competition is tougher." "How the hell can they sell their product at that price?" "Details are maddening." "Accountants, lawyers, and bankers are driving me crazy." "This place needs help." "What do I do?"

We are all searching for help.

Not too long ago, at the National Association of Business's monthly luncheon meeting, I noted that about 250 people were in attendance. The room was rather noisy. People were laughing and talking, and dishes were clanging as busboys cleared the tables. I was at the head table. To my left was Walter Green, chief economist for a major bank. To my right was the program chairman for the event, Bill Watson.

Bill had just mentioned that the attendance for their monthly meetings was normally 150, but because of Walter Green's prominence as an economist, an additional 100 people had come that day. Interesting, I thought, economists have become drawing cards for business meetings, conventions, and seminars. They must be making a fortune!

During lunch Walter and I were chatting about everything and nothing in particular. "Walter, how long will you be speaking?" I asked.

"About 20 minutes," he said.

Not bad, I thought, only 20 minutes of boredom.

After a glowing introduction, Walter went to the podium, and began his talk. A large-framed man of about 6' 3", Walter wore a dull grey suit, the kind so often favored by bankers and politicians who want to look efficient, substantial, and conservative. From time-to time, I glanced at my watch and was surprised to note that Walter had been speaking for 30 minutes and was still going strong. He held the audience well. He was charming, witty, and not at all boring. He was on for another 15 minutes before he concluded and was given an enthusiastic and respectable round of applause. No question about it—Walter's presentation had been successful.

A few days later, I was thinking about some of the items Walter had covered: interest rates, deficits, M-1 money supply, the European economy, the prognosis for the American economy, and so on. Two hundred fifty people had gone to hear Walter's speech, 100 more than the usual NAB luncheon meeting attendance.

Why? What were these people looking for? And why have economists like Walter Green, Arthur Laffer, Milton Friedman, and Eliot Janeway become so popular that people flock to listen to them speak?

The answer is surprisingly simple. People want help. They flock to hear these "business gurus of the 80s," hopeful that somewhere in the theory, buzzwords, and elaborate rationale is an effective strategy for the small and medium-sized business. True, when I heard Walter speak, he was witty, charming, and entertaining. But he said nothing. An extra 100 people had gone to hear him, but they did not get the help they sought. What help is there for us in the proliferation of inconsistent economic theories permeating our society? We run for help, but get wit, charm, entertainment, and confusion. The gurus have failed us. We are left to our own devices.

WHAT CAN WE DO ABOUT IT?

In the pages that follow, I am going to outline some specific steps that get right to the heart of the matter. These steps begin with some key assumptions.

We, the leaders of our business, cannot run our companies on an overabundance of inconsistent economic theories. We cannot run our companies on the theoretical notions of what leadership characteristics we should have. It doesn't matter. We are the leaders, like it or not. We are the people who must make things happen.

We must strive for greater profitability. Of course, product and service are vital factors, but unless we learn how to adequately control the expenses of our business, we are at the mercy of unseen forces.

We must develop a system that allows us to monitor the key financial elements of our companies and we must come to understand what financial numbers really mean.

We must also develop a plan for the future that gives us guidance while it provides us with goals.

Power and influence are vital forces; we must develop as much as necessary to make our voices heard when our interests are at stake.

We must learn how to delegate authority and to train people to perform vital tasks within the organization. We must protect our most valuable asset—our employees.

As far as I'm concerned, the most powerful key assumption of all of this is: We must spend the 122 minutes per month necessary to build a better business.

2
How to Control the Expenses of Your Business

IT WAS 1980, the economy was booming and so was Joel Riordan's manufacturing business. With his company's volume at an all time high, Joel was traveling around the country, hustling to get volume even higher.

That June, Joel, and I and an associate of mine were sitting in our conference room reviewing the financial statements of Joel's company. My associate and I were noting a trend. Sales were strong, but profits weren't where they should be. Expenses were increasing far too rapidly. "Joel, what's going on?" I asked. "Every expense category on your financial statement is growing out of proportion, and we're concerned."

"Accountants," Joel responded. "Our volume is greater than ever, we're on an upswing, and you worry. Too high a profit means too high a tax. I'm just enjoying myself."

In 1981 the economy turned against Joel, and his volume started a steady decline. Six months later we met again. "Joel, you've got to cut the fat out of your company," I said. "You've shown a loss for the last two quarters and the expenses are still high."

Joel responded in his typical manner, "What I need are better sales reps and a better general manager to help me run the company."

"What you really need," I insisted, "is to get those expenses under control, cut down on some travel, stay home, and manage the company."

Joel's sales continued to decline and although he managed to survive the recession of 1981 and 1982, his company took its final breath in 1983. Joel could have saved his company and made a good living, but he had spent himself into so much debt when things were good that he couldn't continue. Joel was not an isolated case. His knock-the-world-dead-with-volume-and-spend,-spend,-spend philosophy is practiced far too often.

Most people involved in small companies spend a great deal of time attempting to increase sales but do little to control operating expenses. Certainly, I wouldn't abandon the notion of increasing volume. But remember that every dollar saved in expenses results in a dollar more in profit. A one-to-one ratio. It may take $10, $15, $20 or even more of increased volume to produce the same one dollar profit. Thus, when you view the profound impact that controlling expenses has on your profitability, it becomes essential that all efforts be made to control the expenses of your business.

HOW CAN I? THREE STEPS!

When I advise clients or groups of small business people to control their expenses, the most common response I hear is defeat. "How can I? Suppliers are constantly hounding us with increases. A day doesn't go by without someone asking for more money."

Expenses can be controlled, but it's up to you. Three steps will lead to greater expense control: Become familiar with the expenses of your business; anticipate in advance what those expenses should be; manage them by exception.

FINANCIAL STATEMENTS SHOULD TELL YOU A STORY

What are the expenses of your business? Be honest with yourself. Do you really know? It is not unusual for owners and managers to be so bogged down in details that they never take the time to review the various expense categories of their business.

What are you spending money on? Just look over your company's financial statements and review the various categories of expenditure. Are they telling you a story? Are you satisfied with the detail? Too little? Too much? It's your company. They are your financial statements and they should tell you what you want and need to know.

DESIGN THEM YOURSELF

Here's an easy way to design financial statements that can be more meaningful to you and tell you the story:

Next time you sign checks, sit down with your bookkeeper and have a detailed list of the company's expense categories available. As you sign each check, ask yourself if you want to know on a regular basis how much you spend for the item the check represents. For example, you sign a $25 check payable to the post office. You know you don't spend much on postage, so you are not concerned. But say the check is for $450. And you're curious about what postage costs on a regular basis. Ask the bookkeeper where this item is on the financial statements. The bookkeeper may tell you, "It's in office supplies." If it's lumped together with all the other items in the category of office supplies, direct the bookkeeper to set up a new category for postage so it will be reflected on your financial statement as a separate item. Now, each time you review your profit and loss, postage will be a separate line item giving you the information you want and need to know.

If you follow this procedure for all the bills being paid, you will develop financial categories that have meaning to you. Remember, the statement must tell *you* what is going on. You are the one who is responsible for the success or failure of the business. Therefore, it is essential to design the categories for your needs, your curiosity, your style. It's your money.

ANTICIPATE WHAT YOUR EXPENSES SHOULD BE

Every business operating in today's economic environment must have a budget. You'll never be able to control expenses if you don't know what they should be. You can spend and spend, but you can't know if you've spent too much if you haven't given any forethought to what you should be spending.

Once you have determined what an operating expense should be and then compared it to what it actually is, you will be in a position to know if you have achieved the goal of controlling expenses.

A THEFT COULD HAVE BEEN PREVENTED

Here is an example of how the process of comparing actual expenses to the budget would have caught a theft in a company early on and possibly could have prevented it altogether.

Joe Scott and Eric Brown had been partners in the manufacturing business for 10 years. They had started on a shoestring yet built their company to its present $8,000,000 per annum sales volume. Profits were consistently high.

Joe was about 10 years older than Eric and had a nasty temper. He controlled the purse strings of the company and frankly was tough to deal with.

Eric's position in the company was in production. He paid little attention to financial matters and seemed only concerned with what his annual salary would be.

The office I was sitting in was cold. Joe always had the air conditioning on too high. He sat behind a beautifully polished Bank of England desk, unaware of my discomfort and vaguely annoyed about the thrust of my request for the meeting.

Eric sat to my right. He also seemed oblivious to the chill, and likewise to Joe's irritation with me. On the desk in front of us were copies of the financial statements of the past two years.

"My reason for this meeting," I said, tapping the most recent statement with my pencil, "is to express concern over the rise in the company's expenses. Compared to recent periods, they seem exceptionally high."

Joe took issue immediately. "Your concerns are unfounded and the figures must be wrong. Call in the bookkeeper."

In a moment we were joined by Sue, the company bookkeeper, a very thin, short woman who always looked as though she had been working for the past twenty-four hours. She was an excellent bookkeeper. "Sue, your numbers are wrong," Joe said.

Sue didn't give an inch. "You always say that, Mr. Scott."

We were at an impasse, and to break it, Sue and I retired to her office to review the ledgers. When we reported that the numbers were indeed right, Joe began to mumble.

"When you spend money," I began, "how do you know if you're going overboard or not?"

"Sue prepares a report," Joe said brusquely.

"But we've just seen what happens when Sue presents the figures. You challenge them, and even when they check out, you don't pay any attention to them. You should be getting information more often, and both of you should compare the actual figures against previous targets. You should do this every month."

For years I had attempted to convince them to use some kind of budget or forecast, and for years, they had passed. We parted with Joe and Eric upbeat. Why not? Profits were good, Eric continued to receive his salary and Joe released some anger. About a week later, Eric Brown, uncharacteristically agitated and concerned, called my office. "That S.O.B. Joe has been paying personal expenses through the business without my knowledge."

No wonder, I thought, that expenses hadn't seemed too high for Joe. "How much?" I asked.

"About $50,000. We're still checking."

We left matters with Eric's promise that he'd call me if Sue's investigations produced any more results. Two days later, Eric was back on the line. "We're up to $75,000" he said.

"Ouch," I said.

"You're telling me," Eric mumbled. We ended our conversation.

Two more days passed before I heard from Eric again. "This year alone, $250,000."

What happened? Neither of the partners were responsible to the company. Joe Scott, with control over the purse strings, was able to spend and spend. Eric, involved only in his production, didn't have any idea where the company was going and where it should be.

Had Joe and Eric reviewed financial data regularly and compared the data to predetermined goals, Joe would have had a difficult time spending company funds on personal expenditures. The variance from expected results would have been glaring enough to support my concern and would have been easily spotted. More than likely, the theft would not have taken place.

3
The Budget Process

THE MAIN PURPOSE of the budget process is to control expenses and set goals. An important budget by-product is to make the information on financial statements significantly more meaningful. How can you assess financial data if you don't know what the numbers should be?

Shell Taper, owner of a small manufacturing company, is an excellent case in point. Recently, when I handed Shell his P & L, it showed a $50,000 profit for the year. Shell looked at it, then asked me, "How do you think I did?"

"A $50,000 profit seems okay, Shell, but we can't really know how you did if we don't know how you *wanted* to do. If you anticipated a $250,000 profit, you did miserably. If you anticipated $10,000, you did quite well. You should be predetermining the results of operations, then when the results are in, you'll know if you're on the right track."

OH MY GOD, THREE!

There are three budgets necessary in the process, but don't become anxious; make it easy on yourself. Get someone else to prepare it for you, get a computer, or do both (see Chapter 6). If you take this approach, you still must be involved in the process at all times, but you delegate the clerical details to others. This may be the bookkeeper who searches for every penny in balancing the accounts or some new hire who wants to impress the boss. Find someone you can trust and let that person assist you in this vital work. You will make all the decisions regarding the budget, the clerk handles the details.

DON'T FORGET A PROFIT

You must not only prepare a budget to chart your progress, you must budget a profit. Treat profit as if it were any other expense of your business. Most people with small companies simply don't have the net worth, resources, or clout to sustain losses, and it certainly makes no sense to budget losses. Even nonprofit organizations budget their operations to break even, and they, too, need to budget their anticipated expenses to avoid any embarassing cash short-fall.

If profit is the name of your game—and I urge you to behave as though it is—you must make reasonable projections for the profit you expect to make. How else will you know how much to charge for your product or service, how much to pay your employees, and how much to pay yourself?

BUDGET NO. 1—THE "PIE IN THE SKY" BUDGET

This budget forecasts high sales, low expenses, and large profits. Generally prepared for bankers and other financiers, it may also be helpful in securing loans or investors—but forget it as a management tool. It's not only a "pie in the sky" budget but also a "who do we think we are kidding?" budget.

By the way, most good financiers will know the game you are playing; don't waste your time. Forget it! Put it in your drawer and leave it there. Our management tool is the next step—Budget No. 2.

BUDGET NO. 2—THE "I HOPE AND PRAY TO GOD I MAKE IT" BUDGET

Achievable sales, honest operating expenses, and reasonable profits: This is reality. The budget we are going to hang our hats on. The one we are going to make all efforts to achieve, so that we never have to use Budget No. 3.

BUDGET NO. 3—THE "I HOPE AND PRAY TO GOD I NEVER USE IT" BUDGET

This is the last ditch budget that will assist you in surviving if you don't reach expected results.

I firmly recommend a survival budget because most people operating a small business generally don't react to change and economic conditions quickly enough. Most large companies hire specialists, who attempt to predict the economic future, and may also employ large staffs to prepare budgets based on predicted trends. This gives them a substantial edge in making it through hard times. We have no such advantage. Our edge is ourselves.

We make economic predictions based on "gut feelings" and "seat of the pants planning." Therefore, it is absolutely necessary for us to react to changing conditions as quickly as possible. What do we do when our loan interest rates jump 4 to 8 points, sales are divided in half, and cash flow dries up? We must prepare for the worst in advance.

The key triggering mechanism for going from a realistic budget to the survival budget is a sudden or steady decline in sales. When things change, your best friend will be your computer. It is designed to allow you to change figures and re-run your company budgets at different levels of, let's say, sales. Thus, if your sales are in decline, you can project the decline for a sustained period of time and, in a very few minutes, have your projected results. This will give you an immediate view of the future and allow for a quick response to changing times.

4
The
I Hate To Budget
Budget

T HE SECRET OF EFFECTIVE budget preparation is to use as little effort as possible. When I have read literature on budget preparation, I have been overwhelmed by mine fields of massive verbiage—fixed costs, variable costs, break-even analysis, assumptions, zero based budget, costs relationships, etc., etc. These complex items confuse and prevent us from focusing on what is important, the budget preparation.

The amount of time you spend will depend on how exact you want the budget to be. If this is your first attempt at budget preparation, don't get yourself involved in being too precise. Concentrate on reasonableness and general ideas. Complex budget preparation can come at a later date. Right now let's just get something on paper to establish next year's financial targets.

In the descriptions that follow, I have simplified the steps enough to allow you to have your bookkeeping personnel prepare most of the details. Your responsibility is determining the methods to be used.

STEP 1—SALES FORECAST

The first step in budget preparation is the sales forecast. Ideally, you should confer with customers, sales managers and/or representatives to project the next year's expected sales. However, many owner-managers find the process of securing the input from others to be rather time-consuming, cumbersome, and offering little accuracy. Here are two methods to help you predict the year's sales.

Alternative 1: Take the previous year's sales dollar volume and add to it the current year's expected price increases and anticipated volume increases. This may be referred to as a "reasonable guess."

Example:

Previous year's sales	$ 1,580,000
Estimated price increases at 7½%	118,500
	$ 1,698,500
Volume increased at 10%	169,850
Expected sales	$ 1,868,350
Use (rounded)	$ 1,870,000

Alternative 2: A more precise method to compute sales dollar volume is to begin with units of product to be sold during the year, then convert units sold to a dollar value. Remember, if you compute sales by product and prepare this forecast for each month's quantities to be sold, it will be far more accurate than a "reasonable guess."

Example:

Unit Sales Previous year		This year* increase	Total Units	Unit** Price	Total
Product A	50,000	10,000	60,000	11.50	$ 690,000
Product B	35,000	2,000	37,000	20.00	740,000
Product C	100,000	17,000	117,000	3.75	438,750
Expected sales					$1,868,750
Use (rounded)					$1,870,000

*more reasonable guessing
**include price increases

STEP 2—SALES: MONTH-BY-MONTH ANALYSIS

Once you have determined the dollar amount to be used for your expected sales, you must then project how the sales will be produced on a month-by-month basis. This step gives you tight financial control and is accomplished in one of two ways:

Alternative 1: Predict each month's sales and use the result. This method is simple to use and can be of great value if you gather enough data to predict with accuracy.

Alternative 2: Assume that the relationship of each month's sales to the year's total sales will be the same each year. Thus, if last January's sales were 10 percent of last year's total sales, then we can assume that in our current budget year, January sales will be 10 percent of the year's total. Review the prior year or past years' sales, month-by-month, to determine the relationship of each month's sales in your budget to the annual sales. This method may lack some accuracy, however, it is simple to use.

Example:

Prior year's sales		% to Total	Expected Sales	Monthly Sales	%
January	$ 100,000	6.9 ×	1,870,000	$ 129,030	6.9
February	100,000	6.9 ×	1,870,000	129,030	6.9
March	100,000	6.9 ×	1,870,000	129,030	6.9
April	100,000	6.9 ×	1,870,000	129,030	6.9
May	150,000	10.3 ×	1,870,000	192,610	10.3
June	150,000	10.3 ×	1,870,000	192,610	10.3
July	125,000	8.7 ×	1,870,000	162,690	8.7
August	100,000	6.9 ×	1,870,000	129,030	6.9
September	150,000	10.3 ×	1,870,000	192,610	10.3
October	100,000	6.9 ×	1,870,000	129,030	6.9
November	125,000	8.7 ×	1,870,000	162,690	8.7
December	150,000	10.3 ×	1,870,000	192,610	10.3
Total	$1,450,000	100.0		$1,870,000	100.0%

STEP 3—COST OF GOODS SOLD

The next item to be considered in our budget is the cost of goods sold—how much you pay for what you sell.

I have listed two basic methods for determining the cost of goods sold. Pick the one you find the simplest and use it.

Alternative 1: The Percentage Method. Let's assume that over the years your business has been operating on a consistent cost of goods sold percentage. Let's further assume that you would like to continue to operate at the same level for the coming year. Simply multiply that percent by each month's sales; the result becomes the cost of sales for the month. This method may prove to be the simplest way to budget costs of goods sold; however, its major weakness will be discovered when the actual costs are more or less than the budget, and you try to find out why.

Unlike most of the expenses of your business, the actual cost of goods sold can vary depending on several factors: an incorrect beginning inventory, sales recorded in the wrong period, purchases recorded in the wrong period, an incorrect ending inventory, improper valuation of the inventory and an inaccurate count of the items in the inventory. Therefore, if you have a variance between the actual percent of cost of goods sold compared to the estimated percent used in the budget, pinpointing the reason for the variance can be quite difficult.

In general, a company will not compute the actual cost of goods sold until an accurate physical inventory is taken or reliable perpetual inventory records are maintained. Therefore, management may prepare their actual financial statements using the budgeted cost of goods sold and will not compute the actual cost of goods sold more than once or twice a year when inventories are taken. Only when the actual is computed can meaningful comparisons between actual and budgeted cost of goods sold take place.

Alternative 2: For a more precise method of determining your cost of goods sold budget, begin with the number of units of a particular product that you anticipate selling (see sales forecast alternative 2) and price the units to be sold.

Do this for each product line of sales.

Example:

Units to Be Sold		Anticipated Cost of Each Unit	Cost of Goods Sold
Product A	50,000	$ 7.80	$ 390,000
Product B	35,000	$ 12.75	446,250
Product C	100,000	$ 1.25	125,000
Cost of Goods Sold			$ 961,250

STEP 4—EXPENSES

Here is a list of the expense items generally found on most financial statements followed by brief comments on how these items may be budgeted for the year. This list is not all inclusive; you may have items on your financial statements not shown here. Any items of importance to you should be reflected on your financial statements.

Advertising: If advertising is not a major expenditure, compute your budget amount by using the prior year's advertising expense percentage of sales to the current year's predicted sales. This percent should be applied to each month. If advertising is a significant expense, consider establishing your budget in conjunction with your ad agency.

Automobile expense: Estimate a reasonable cost for operating a car during the year and multiply that cost by the number of company cars. This will give you your annual expenditures. To arrive at the monthly expenditure, divide this number by twelve.

While you are in the process of counting cars, you might consider whether the company needs as many cars as it is currently paying for, whether you may be able to use less expensive automobiles, or whether you should lease. Be sure to figure in all insurance, interest payments, repairs, and maintenance. If you do opt for leasing, all payments should be included in the budget. Don't forget the new IRS recordkeeping requirements.

Bad debts: Review historical data to track bad debts as a percentage of sales. Take your historical percentage and apply it to the sales for each month in your budget. If you believe the percentage is excessive, a reduced budgeted percent may be in order. However, try to be realistic; now may be the time to review credit policies, put some delinquent accounts on a cash only basis, and cut off others completely. Develop a consistent policy and stick to it (see Chapter 7).

Business promotion: Take the number of people in the company who are in sales functions, mutiply that by the number of dollars you consider appropriate for each person to be spending for promotion during the ensuing year, and compute promotion as a percentage of sales. Apply that percent for every month of the budget. Or just take the annual amount and divide it by twelve and apply the 1/12 to each month of the budget. Don't forget the new recordkeeping requirements of the IRS.

Collection costs: Because accounts receivable are getting tougher to collect, you should consider budgeting some additional dollars for collections during the year.

The best way to determine the amount would be to review what percentage of sales the collection costs have been running historically and apply that percentage to each month's sales. You may want to budget additional costs if you plan on taking a hard-line approach to collections (see Chapter 7).

Continuing education: This is an area where few small companies spend significant dollars. After you've read this book, I hope you will have been convinced to spend more (see Chapter 10 for suggestions).

To determine your budget, review the people in your organization and see which ones might benefit from continuing education. Don't forget to include yourself. Multiply the number of people by the dollars decided for each. This will be your annual expense. For simplification in applying the dollar amounts to the monthly budgets, just divide the total allocation by twelve.

Depreciation: This item is purely a function of methods that you are already using for tax purposes. Take your annual amount, divide it by twelve, and apply this amount to each month of the budget.

If your tax depreciation produces an excessive expenditure, consider using a different method for financial statements. Longer useful lives with lower depreciation rates will enhance your financial statements and present a better picture to whoever uses the statements.

Donations: This, too, should be budgeted. Decide on your annual amount, stick to it, and if you think you may want to add an extra amount for unanticipated causes, by all means do so, but do it in the beginning of the budget year. For your monthly budget divide by twelve and apply the amount to each month of the budget.

Dues and subscriptions: Now is the time to make certain that all those organizations you've joined and publications you subscribe to are of benefit to your company. Then, look at the previous year and add for increased costs. If you are anticipating some additional expenditures in this area you should certainly budget them at this time. Apply 1/12 to each month of the budget.

Insurance: General insurance is the cost of insuring equipment, liability, etc. Call your insurance agent and find out exactly what you should anticipate in insurance premiums for the year. Use this amount for your budget. Or, if you are consistently paying the same amount from year to year, look at the prior year's financial statements and use that number plus some percentage increase. To do this for your monthly budget, divide by twelve and apply the amount to each month of the budget.

While reviewing your budget, you should be determining whether your coverage is adequate. A complete review of your insurance program at this time may save dollars.

Group insurance: There are several items that will be based on the number of employees you have in your organization. To determine these items you must budget the number of employees you anticipate having in the next twelve months on a month-by-month basis. This will require you to plan when you will be adding or possibly reducing your personnel. To budget your group insurance, take the number of employees each month, multiply that by the group insurance rate, and you have your budget.

Life insurance is generally an item confined to a few people in the organization. Have your bookkeeper call your insurance agent and find out what you should be budgeting for life insurance. Do your monthly budget by taking the annual cost and dividing by twelve, or ask your agent when the premiums are due and place it on your budget on the due dates. The life insurance industry has developed many new products over the past few years. Have your coverage analyzed to see if costs can be reduced.

Interest expense: This item depends on what you are going to be borrowing and what the interest rates are going to be in the future. It is best to anticipate high when it comes to interest, therefore, when you review your cash requirements, project high, a 20 to 30 percent increase over the previous year may be in order. Keep your fingers crossed that it won't happen. Only God and the chairman of the Federal Reserve Board can tell us where interest rates will be going. One-twelfth a month of the total will give you a reasonable budget.

Legal and accounting: To determine your budget for legal and accounting, ask your lawyer and accountant what they anticipate your costs will be during the year. If you feel that their anticipated fees are high, negotiations may be in order.

Office supplies and postage: Sometimes this can be a tough category to anticipate. Go back and look at what the annual percent has been running for the past few years; apply that percent on a month-by-month basis to your budget. Also consider whether the percent has been reasonable in the past and whether you feel you may be able to reduce it. Generally, historical percentage is the best method for budgeting this item.

Rent: This budgeted number is easy. Just use your montly rent figure for each month of the budget. Don't forget any cost of living increases, mall charges, or property tax and expense escalations.

Repairs and maintenance: Review the annual percent over the past few years and apply that percentage on a month-by-month basis to each month's sales.

Don't forget to include contracts for preventive maintenance. Now may be the time to consider whether to upgrade and improve equipment that requires constant maintenance.

Salaries: This item is not difficult to budget if you prepare for it by thinking through your plans for each employee for the next twelve months. My suggestion for budgeting salaries is to literally count the numbers of employees you anticipate each month. Add up each employee's anticipated monthly salary and you have your budget for the year.

Remember to budget approximate salary increases. If you have a large number of employees, tell your bookkeeper to prepare schedules, but the basic policies should come from you.

While you're reviewing salaries, you should consider developing standard policies for sick leave, vacation, holidays, and other fringe benefits. Are your company's policies communicated in an employee manual? This is a must. It will prevent confusion, conflict, and even lawsuits.

Taxes and licenses: Determine the historical percentage and apply that factor to the current year. Check appropriate city, state, and federal sources for potential increases. Divide by twelve and apply it to each month of the budget.

Taxes, Payroll: This should be budgeted by taking a percentage— anywhere from 10 to 15 percent—of the gross payroll cost as your monthly budget.

Telephone and utilities: Check prior years' records to get a rough estimate of the percentage of sales. Apply this percentage to each month, add 10 to 15 percent to this number. Another method is to take the prior year's dollars, add 10 to 15 percent to that number and divide by twelve to determine each month's expense.

Travel: Increasing travel costs make it necessary to plan realistically and early. If you anticipate extensive travel, this is the time to sit down and decide what trips will be taken, where you will be traveling, and who will be going. Develop a written travel policy. Avoid travel by whim.

If your company travel plans are modest, take the total annual dollars and divide by twelve to determine your monthly budget. If you project extensive traveling, I recommend that you calculate each month separately by the actual anticipated trips for the given month.

Company travel can result in employee abuse of the privilege. Make certain adequate documentation is available after each trip. This will result in controlled costs and fewer headaches with the IRS.

Look closely at trips to conventions and trade shows. Are they necessary, or are they just social gatherings?

YOUR COMPANY'S BUDGET

The following pages illustrate a simple budget using the alternatives and headings I have outlined in the previous section. To simplify the preparation of your own budget, make a list of each profit and loss item with an appropriate budget assumption. After you have done this, you can delegate the rest of the task. The balance is entirely clerical.

BUDGET ASSUMPTIONS

Mary — use these numbers.

Category   **Assumptions**

Sales: alternative 1 from Book up your cash flow

Cost of goods sold: use 45% of sales

Advertising: 5% of sales

Automobile: Company has 4 autos @ 1500 ea.
4 × 1500 = 6000 ÷ 12 = 500 per month

Bad debts: maintain @ 2% of sales — I hope!

Business promotion: Prior year was 65000. 10% increase
equals $71500 ÷ 12

Collection costs: use 1000 per month

Continuing education: $1000 per month

Depreciation: $84000 per year — use 7000 per month

Donations: $10,000 per year = ÷ 12

Insurance—general: agent said $24000; use 2000 per month

Insurance—group: 15 employees @ 1500 ea = 22500 ÷ 12 =
monthly #.

Insurance—life: 600 per month

Interest: expect to borrow 250M @ 15% = 37,500 ÷ 12
= 3125 per month + other borrowings.

Office supplies: 2% of sales — and keep it there please!

Rent: 4000 per month

Repairs and maintenance: use 400 per month

Salaries: schedule the payroll per month

Taxes and license: Prior years was 1.5% of sales use same
this year.

Taxes, payroll: 20% of monthly payroll

Telephone—utilities: $29000 last year. Use 33000 ÷ 12
Travel — use $1000 per month.

COMPANY BUDGET
FOR PERIOD JANUARY TO DECEMBER

	Jan.	Feb.	Mar.	Apr.	May
Sales	$ 129,030	$ 129,030	$ 129,030	$ 129,030	$ 192,610
Cost of Sales @ 45%	58,063	58,063	58,063	58,063	86,675
Gross profit	70,967	70,967	70,967	70,967	105,935
Advertising @ 5%	6,450	6,450	6,450	6,450	9,600
Automobile	500	500	500	500	500
Bad debts @ 2%	2,580	2,580	2,580	2,580	3,840
Business promotions	5,958	5,958	5,958	5,958	5,958
Collection costs	1,000	1,000	1,000	1,000	1,000
Continuing education	1,000	1,000	1,000	1,000	1,000
Depreciation	7,000	7,000	7,000	7,000	7,000
Donations	833	833	833	833	833
Dues & subscriptions	833	833	833	833	833
Insurance—general	2,000	2,000	2,000	2,000	2,000
Insurance—group	1,875	1,875	1,875	1,875	1,875
Insurance—life	600	600	600	600	600
Interest	3,125	3,125	3,125	3,125	4,375
Legal & accounting	1,000	1,000	1,000	1,000	1,000
Office supplies @ 2%	2,580	2,580	2,580	2,580	3,840
Rent	4,000	4,000	4,000	4,000	4,000
Repairs	400	400	400	400	400
Salaries	21,000	21,000	21,000	21,000	21,000
Taxes & license @ 1.5%	1,935	1,935	1,935	1,935	2,880
Taxes, payroll	4,200	4,200	4,200	4,200	4,200
Telephone—utilities	2,750	2,750	2,750	2,750	2,750
Travel	1,000	1,000	1,000	1,000	1,000
Total	72,619	72,619	72,619	72,619	80,484
Profit	$ (1,652)	$ (1,652)	$ (1,652)	$ (1,652)	$ 25,451

	Jun.	Jul.	Aug.	Sep.	Oct.	Nov.	Dec.	Total
	$ 192,610	$ 162,690	$ 129,030	$ 192,610	$ 129,030	$ 162,690	$ 192,610	$ 1,870,000
	86,675	73,211	58,063	86,675	58,063	73,211	86,675	841,500
	105,935	89,479	70,967	105,935	70,967	89,479	105,935	1,028,500
	9,600	8,100	6,450	9,600	6,450	8,100	10,050	93,750
	500	500	500	500	500	500	500	6,000
	3,840	3,240	2,580	3,840	2,580	3,240	3,920	37,400
	5,958	5,958	5,958	5,958	5,958	5,958	5,962	71,500
	1,000	1,000	1,000	1,000	1,000	1,000	1,000	12,000
	1,000	1,000	1,000	1,000	1,000	1,000	1,000	12,000
	7,000	7,000	7,000	7,000	7,000	7,000	7,000	84,000
	833	833	833	833	833	833	837	10,000
	833	833	833	833	833	833	837	10,000
	2,000	2,000	2,000	2,000	2,000	2,000	2,000	24,000
	1,875	1,875	1,875	1,875	1,875	1,875	1,875	22,500
	600	600	600	600	600	600	600	7,200
	4,375	4,375	4,450	4,450	4,450	4,450	4,450	47,875
	1,000	1,000	1,000	1,000	1,000	1,000	1,000	12,000
	3,840	3,240	2,580	3,840	2,580	3,240	3,920	37,400
	4,000	4,000	4,000	4,000	4,000	4,000	4,000	48,000
	400	400	400	400	400	400	400	4,800
	21,000	24,833	24,833	24,833	24,833	24,833	24,835	275,000
	2,880	2,430	1,935	2,880	1,935	2,430	2,890	28,000
	4,200	4,966	4,966	4,966	4,966	4,966	4,970	55,000
	2,750	2,750	2,750	2,750	2,750	2,750	2,750	33,000
	1,000	1,000	1,000	1,000	1,000	1,000	1,000	12,000
	80,484	81,933	78,543	85,158	78,543	82,008	85,796	943,425
	$ 25,451	$ 7,546	$ (7,576)	$ 20,777	$ (7,576)	$ 7,471	$ 20,139	$ 85,075

5
What Do You Do with Your Budget Now That You Have One?

YOU NOW HAVE the best tool available for managing your business and controlling expenses. On a monthly basis, compare the operations of your company with the budget on a line-by-line basis.

As you make your monthly check, you will be able to locate differences between what you thought would happen and what actually did happen. This helps enormously. Now you can avoid being a crisis manager; you can confine your management activities to the exceptions, items that are significantly different from the budget.

In my organization, there was an extended period when our office supplies (a large expense in a professional office) never came within budget. I made numerous inquiries and of course the administrator always had some plausible explanation. Even so, we consistently overshot the budget for office supplies.

After continued frustration, I suggested we check out some other sources for our supplies. You guessed it. Our friendly vendor was 20 to 30 percent higher than his competitor. Now the expense is under control. That's what this is all about—keeping expenses under control.

You don't have to shake your head in bewilderment. Ask questions; then keep on asking until you get the answers you need to keep within the framework you've provided in your budget.

WHAT IF THE BUDGET IS WRONG?

Change it! A budget is a living document which changes as conditions change. We use the budget to establish achievable and realistic goals. It is not for playing games with ourselves by establishing ideals that make no sense in the real world.

After you have reviewed particular items for a number of months, and have taken corrective action and are still consistently over or under the budget, correct the budget. But remember: A budget change should only be made *after* you have exhausted all remedies to bring your actual expenses or income in line with your original estimates. It is important to change the budget so you can have a meaningful analysis of where you are headed.

ARE YOU SATISFIED?

One of the most important items in the preparation of your budget is your compensation and the profit you have allowed or budgeted for your company. Make certain that the salary you have established for yourself and the profits are adequate. It makes no sense to work for peanuts. Making a reasonable salary and a reasonable profit is why you're in business.

If your salary and profit do not meet your expectations, you must give thought to whether your goals are realistic or not. A budget must be based on an honest assessment of what you think you can achieve in the coming period. Take whatever action is necessary to achieve your desired objectives. Success or failure is your responsibility.

Controlling expenses means you must design meaningful financial statements, compare actual against anticipated costs, manage the exception rather than the rule, and ask appropriate questions to get sufficient information to make your business decisions. If you do so you will be in a better position to:

- Evaluate business activities
- Decide where to cut costs
- Monitor your financial successes
- Understand the nature of your operation and the consequences of your decisions
- Be in a better position to react to economic conditions quickly
- Become a better manager
- Make more money

6
A New Life Partner

QUESTION: Should you use a small business computer to assist you in the budget process? Answer: Absolutely! Spreadsheet packages such as VisiCalc, SuperCalc, and Lotus 1-2-3, are great. One word of caution: If you have never used a computer before, you will find that they are quite mesmerizing. You may become so fascinated with their speed and ability you may want to *play* with it. I've seen very high-priced and valuable executives get so involved with the computer that they have wasted valuable time screwing around with the machine. So be careful. Your time is best spent leading your company in the direction you have chosen.

MAKE YOUR COMPUTER PURCHASE SUCCESSFUL

Those of you who will be purchasing a computer, accept my congratulations on your new "marriage." Consummated by the signing of the contract, you have acquired a new life partner.

Consider the parallels. Like some marriages, this union is not bound by love but may be held together because you are at the mercy of the computer company, especially if you were not aware of *all* the facts before making this important commitment. If the relationship that develops between you and the computer company is not a good one, it will probably result in a separation, only to be resolved by attorneys and maybe a visit to court.

Some words of extreme caution. Once you have committed to

this marriage, you will find that your dealer's technical back-up people probably will drive you crazy. They will cajole, cheat, and lie to avoid spending time on your computer system once the bill is paid.

Don't be discouraged. You can be somewhat protected, but before elaborating on how to maintain your sanity and independence in this relationship, let's determine whether or not your company should computerize at all.

DO YOU NEED A COMPUTER?

You may have heard of the $600 wonder machine that is going to revolutionize your life by computerizing all company procedures. If you are a victim of a Madison Avenue campaign, convinced that $600 is the magic number, don't bother to read on. The cost of a good computer system depends on many factors, but be prepared to spend $5,000 to $20,000 if your company is relatively small, or $100,000 or more for larger and more sophisticated companies.

If your company is disorganized, your business a mess, your internal controls weak, if you don't receive financial data and have lost control of some of your activities, you have management problems. The computer won't solve these problems: it will only add to them. It cannot create form out of chaos.

Begin with a realistic attitude. Be prepared to spend the time and money required, and remember the computer is merely a tool to assist you in management decisions; it will not solve your problems by itself.

Go through the following steps to determine whether your business should computerize.

STEP 1—ANALYZE AND DIAGRAM THE PAPERFLOW OF YOUR COMPANY

I am not suggesting that the president of your company start flow-charting his own business, but I am suggesting it should be done by someone. This does not need to be anything complicated: just a diagram reflecting the flow of paper through your company. You may find those procedures cumbersome to chart, but you must have the knowledge of your systems before you can computerize. Without this knowledge, you are headed for mistakes in defining your actual computer requirements.

Review sales invoices and order entry, purchase orders, accounts payable, accounts receivable, payroll, check writing, cash receipts, inventory control, cost accounting, time analysis and/or client cost accounting.

STEP 2— IMPROVE EXISTING PROCEDURES BEFORE YOU CONVERT TO DATA PROCESSING

You must have an accounting system that is operating correctly before you attempt to integrate a computer into your operation. The computer will not create a better system; it will only process the existing system. You've heard it thousands of times, "garbage in, garbage out." You must have an accounting system that is operating correctly before you attempt to integrate a computer into your operation.

STEP 3—ASK YOURSELF TWO QUESTIONS: WHAT DO I WANT THE COMPUTER TO DO? WHAT DO I WANT THE COMPUTER TO TELL ME?

Make a list of every vital function within your organization. Check off the ones you want the computer to do for you, then review your list to see if you've been specific enough. I wanted the computer in my organization to be able to issue reports on the ratio of expenses to profits. All concerned agreed that this was a valuable task for the computer to perform. One partner suggested the computer give us the information in graphics as well. We welcomed the idea of having a bar graph and a slice-of-the-pie graph to show these vital statistics.

A client of ours, heavily involved in sales to individuals, wanted her computer to be able to do a newsletter. A private school we advised wanted the computer it bought to keep attendance records, and of course numerous clients wanted the computer to keep an up-to-the-minute inventory. Some of our manufacturing clients wanted their computer to tell them when they should re-order certain components.

Get the point? Every process you want computerized should be described in as much detail as necessary to give you a picture of what reports you expect after it's installed. Typical processes computerized are: accounts receivable, payroll, sales, vacation schedules, order entry, accounts payable, inventory, customer lists, and financial holdings.

Once you know what processes you want the computer to do, you must determine what you want to find out from the process. Do you, for instance, want the process to merely carry an inventory, or do you want to be alerted when the inventory falls below a certain point? Do you want the computer to tell you which accounts are due, or which ones are 60 days past due? Would you like your computer to keep running tabs on your customers so that you can give them a surprise sales incentive bonus when their dollar volume exceeds a certain plateau?

Making this list and asking these questions has the indirect benefit of causing you to define your management course more sharply; it has the direct effect of describing for you what you expect from a significant piece of equipment you are about to buy.

More important, you are now prepared to specify *in the contract* precisely what the programs must process and which reports the computer must produce. This is essential. You don't want to sign a contract for a $15,000 computer that will be delivered "with the pharmacy package" or "with the XYZ package." You must know what the package (program) will do and what it will tell you (reports). And this must be clearly indicated by including your requirements in the contract.

POINTS TO REMEMBER

If a computer is indicated for your organization, there are certain points to remember about computerization whether you buy or lease.

- You must have employee participation.

- The computer is not going to replace people: it may even add people.
- Someone in your organization must be involved with your data system on a daily basis. That person must be capable of understanding your computer system and must be responsible for its operation.
- Buying or leasing a computer is a time-consuming task. Take your time: don't rush. "Marry in haste. Repent at leisure."
- If you feel your business is getting out of hand, you may need a total in-house reorganization before automating. You may be experiencing managerial problems, not problems that can be corrected by data processing.
- Determine your computer requirements yourself or with outside consultants who sell neither hardware nor software. Independent evaluation is a must. Do not rely on the vendor. They have a vested interest in your buying their system.

WHICH SYSTEM?

Even though you have defined your computer needs, this does not guarantee a successful installation.

- If this is your first experience with computerization, you will have to learn about a new industry, its technology, and its jargon. Nevertheless, spend most of your time concentrating on what the computer will produce for *your* needs.
- If the vendors' representatives will be providing your computer education, you must work through and evaluate the competing claims of various salespeople. Even the most knowledgeable salespeople are paid to sell and not to teach; thus you should accommodate for gaps in your computer education.
- The decreasing sales prices of today's computers can actually work against you. As those prices have dropped, vendor gross profits have decreased, and the after-sale service of some vendors has declined. If your vendor decides to cut after-sale expenditures on the grounds they aren't justified for such a "minimal" sales price, you may be in trouble.

From your standpoint, the investment may not seem to be "minimal." It will include these items;

- initial hardware (equipment) costs, which are frequently understated if the "total price" quoted does not include sales tax, insurance, installation charges and so on (worse yet, if you buy a system that is too small or the wrong system for your business, you can expect subsequent outlays for hardware);
- software (program) costs, which, if you bought the standard "XYZ package," may include substantial expenditures for modifications done on an hourly-rate basis; and
- the costs incurred by the disruption that can accompany implementation (this is often the largest cost and can include overtime for employees and lost sales attributable to downtime);
- special electrical wiring, personnel training, insurance, and so on.

These interruptions and unexpected expenses can result in bad feelings between you and your vendor. In fact, computer litigation is one of the fastest growing fields of law.

BUILD A BETTER RELATIONSHIP

There are steps you can take to build a better relationship between you and the vendor:

Be patient. For a microcomputer with one to two terminals, allow two to four months to get the computer installed in-house with some applications up and running. A large minicomputer installation could take nine to eighteen months. You must be patient.

Build your relationship on a solid foundation, give each vendor your request for proposal (RFP), a *written* document outlining your needs. Allowing the vendors to make assumptions about your needs will be your biggest mistake. If you call in ten vendors and simply *tell* them your needs, each one will leave with different facts and assumptions. Then, when you get their responses, you will be comparing apples to oranges.

A REQUEST FOR PROPOSAL (RFP)

A properly structured RFP will include the following sections and must be based on your defined computer requirements:

- the background information on your company, such as company history (where you have been) and company philosophy (where you are going, including growth assumptions), the applications that will require automating, and the priorities assigned to the different applications;

- specific definitions of the software applications, consisting of (a) descriptions of the applications (even a basic application like accounts receivable has different meanings for different people); (b) the features desired (for example, the ability to give extended dating and age properly on accounts receivable); (c) the reports required by management (indicate the frequency and content of all reports and, if a particular report is unique to the industry, attach an example); and (d) your processing volumes (like the number of customers, number of invoices in a month, average number of days of your outstanding invoices);

- your RFP should require the vendor to supply the following information: technical requirements such as the description of the equipment and its capacity limits, the number of training hours you will receive, delivery dates, the vendor's maintenance capabilities, names of at least 10 previous customers, examples of all reports in their proposed packages, the trade-in value of the equipment (if you need to upgrade), changes you must make in your facilities (air-conditioning and electrical), and whether any lawsuits are pending against the vendor.

The vendors will need time to think about your system and may need three to four weeks to reply to your RFP.

Once you receive the vendors' proposal, review two basic areas: hardware and software/service. Give these areas different weight in your evaluation. Hardware should represent 33 percent of the final decision, and software/service should represent 67 percent. The choice of software is *twice* as important as the choice of hardware: most problems on a computer system result from poorly chosen software, usually resulting from poorly defined requirements.

SOFTWARE

Since the choice of a computer comes down to the choice of software, if you choose the wrong software, you are in for many problems. There is a vast difference in purchasing software for a small business, which will more than likely use a microcomputer, and a larger business, which may use either a larger micro, a minicomputer, or a mainframe.

MICRO SOFTWARE

Micro or personal computer software is usually purchased in off-the-shelf packages. These packages will provide general accounting, billing, spreadsheet applications, scheduling, word processing, and data base programs. The packages have a wide distribution and most of the bugs have been worked out. Small businesses can purchase these packages in retail stores, through mail order houses or from independent vendors.

The packages are sold to be used as is, therefore, your company's procedures must conform to the program purchased. This is not difficult for a small, uncomplicated business. It *can* become quite difficult if you have unusual needs. You may need to hire a vendor to write separate programs to deal with your unusual needs.

Packaged software *must* fit your needs. Compare your written list to the output produced by the packaged software. Make certain you're getting what you *want* and *need*.

LARGE MICRO OR MINICOMPUTER SOFTWARE

Locate a standard package that most closely meets your needs and modify it. Do not start from scratch. You should not be paying for custom software applications that are available in standard packages.

Most standard packages were written to meet most generally

used features so some modification will be necessary to fit your company. Try to keep the modification level to less than 10 percent. If you have to modify more than 10 percent of a particular package, don't buy it!

Try to analyze software. Compare each vendor's proposal with your RFP. Itemize the differences. Your goal at this time is to narrow your selection to two or three units which deserve closer scrutiny.

You *must* have access to the system documentation and source code. This may be the only way to save your sanity and keep some degree of independence in this major transaction.

Most computer vendors will tell you that if your software is written in commonly used language, you won't have problems finding other programmers for your system. They fail to tell you that this is possible *only* if you have adequate system documentation; the blueprints of the system (software). Without this, it is virtually impossible for a programmer to get into your system and work on it. Only the dealer has the system documentation, and if he should be out of business, you may be, too.

HARDWARE

Some things to remember about buying hardware:

- An off-brand won't have as much software available and the company may not survive during the shake-out of computer manufacturers.

- It should have a widely used operating system, not a hybrid or one developed especially for their own brand.

- It should have adequate capacity for growth. What is its present memory and disk capacity and what are its limits? At what point will you have to upgrade? Will the upgrade require new equipment or will you be able to add on to the existing system? How much will the upgrade cost?

    Use a 60 percent test. Your initial requirements should never be over 60 percent of the top limit of the system. If the system has a maximum of five CRTs (screens or terminals), you should only need three initially or you will soon need to buy a larger system.

- You should also be certain the system is multi-user (so that more than one person can work on the system at the same time) and multi-task (two or more people can work on different program applications at the same time, *i.e.*, one person works on the payroll, while another person is working on the accounts receivable.)

As you analyze the hardware, evaluate the printer (the component most likely to break down because it has the most moving parts), the facility requirements (changes you must make to accommodate the equipment), and length of warranty. You should also read the user ratings published by one of the independent outside services, such as Data Pro.

SERVICE

In reviewing service, the focus is on the vendor. Consider the following:

- How long will you be covered by the software warranty? Some programs may not be used for the first time until a year after the system is installed (such as preparing W-2 forms for Income Tax). For that reason, a twelve-month or longer warranty should be provided. In some cases it may be better to delay the purchase of some software until you are ready to install it, then have your guarantee run from the later date.

- What is the vendor's previous experience with your type of business? Manufacturing is vastly different from distributing. You do not need to be a guinea pig for a vendor who is unfamiliar with your type of operation. It will be aggravating and frustrating.

- Ask the vendor for references and call them. Talk to the people who run the equipment, not just the owners. You will be surprised what you will learn. If possible, visit an installation.

- Investigate the financial stability of the vendor. The greater the vendor's personal investment in his company, the more likely he is to be stable.

- How fast does the vendor provide maintenance support, and how effective is it? What is the ratio of service reps to the number of installations done by the vendor? Can they provide a back-up facility, and do they offer preventive maintenance?
- Have the vendor's programmers been with them long? What is the ratio of programming staff to installations?
- Will the training be done by a specialist or by a salesperson who would rather be selling, or a programmer who would rather be programming?
- Did the vendor quote only the cost for hardware and software, or did they include all costs, such as sales tax, freight, insurance, installation charges, and supplies? These additional expenses can add up.

CHOOSING THE VENDOR

After you review the areas of hardware, software, and service, rate the vendors and choose the top three (see the vendor rating schedule). If their ratings are close, listen to your intuition. The intangibles are important such as having a good rapport with a particular vendor and his technical people.

Invite each of the vendors to separately tour your business. While they are there, provide each vendor with sample data (invoices, checks, general ledger entries, etc.) to be input into their computer for the demonstration. They can then tailor their demonstrations to meet your requirements.

When viewing a demonstration, take your bookkeeper and the person who will be operating the equipment with you. Do not be detoured by bells and whistles. Remember to emphasize your needs. If the machine malfunctions, take the hint. And remember the salesperson's vested interest: a 5 to 15 percent commission.

The final ratings are usually very close. Review the software and service sections of the vendors' proposals. Don't count pennies. An additional $1,000 means little when you are making this investment.

Price and applications are not all there is to it. Negotiate for other items. If you have heard a particular programmer has an excellent reputation, specify in the contract that he or she will be assigned to your company and include your right to approve any substitution of staff on your account.

Once you make your decision, have an attorney versed in computer law write a rough contract. Never sign a vendor's stock contract. List your computer requirements specifically. Get system documentation. Include "back out" clauses (so that you can back out of the transaction if the vendor fails to meet your specifications) and "hold back" clauses (holding back final payment until you are 100 percent satisfied with the system).

THE LAST STEPS

Before any programming begins, have the vendor prepare a specifications manual that will show you what every screen and report will look like. Have the reports reviewed by the individual most familiar with that information. If changes must be made, have them included in the specifications manual and initialled by you and the vendor. This eliminates many differences that might arise later.

Before you accept delivery, test the software completely (every screen and every report). Do not get impatient. Test the usual and the unusual. Eliminate the bugs as much as possible. Be sure the documentation has been updated, if necessary, and that operating manuals are delivered. Remember: once you accept delivery, you will be a second-class citizen.

In spite of all your precautions, there will be aggravations and frustrations. The first 90 days will be rough, so prepare your personnel for it. Run simultaneous applications, in parallel at first, with your existing system. Go slow. Put on one application at a time, with the most important applications going on first, so the computer can begin to pay for itself.

As you apply this material to your *own* business, take heart. If you have followed the guidelines, organized your procedures before computerizing, chosen the appropriate equipment, negotiated a strong contract, and have been thorough in your implementation, you will have eliminated many of the complications associated with computer- ization. You will receive management information that can improve profitablity; your procedures will be streamlined, and the system will pay for itself in a very short time.

Equally important to your business and nervous system, you will have done your part in your relationship with the vendor and reduced the chances of a "romance gone wrong."

On the following pages, I have included a copy of The Vendor Questionnaire my company provides for its clients, which was devel- oped while selecting and purchasing our own computer system. The Vendor Questionnaire summarizes this chapter, helps you make one of the most vital decisions in your business activities, and serves as a role model for questionnaires you may wish to develop on your own for use in dealing with other suppliers and vendors.

Make photocopies of this questionnaire for all those in your organization who will join you in your computer decision.

THE VENDOR QUESTIONNAIRE

	VENDORS			
	1	2	3	4

I. VENDOR EVALUATION

A. Experience and Client Satisfaction

1. Does the vendor take full responsibility for the complete installation, or are third parties involved?

2. How long has the vendor been in business?

3. How many computer installations has the vendor completed in your area?

4. How many of those installations were in the same industry as your company (with comparable software applications and hardware configuration)?

5. Does the vendor sell mainly to small and medium-sized businesses such as yours? (There is a certain expertise required for a successful installation in a small business.)

6. Are they a full-service vendor? Will they have to refer you to various subcontractors for related services, or can they provide all of the following themselves?

   a. Hardware

   b. Software

   c. Training

   d. Forms Development

   e. Maintenance Service

   f. Support

	VENDORS			
	1	2	3	4

7. Obtain a customer reference list of the installations in Item 4. Then call each of them, asking questions such as these:

   a. Was the salesperson involved in the installation or just taking the order?

   b. Were the programs delivered essentially "bug free"?

   c. What are the strongpoints and the deficiencies of the vendor's maintenance program?

   d. What is their evaluation of the system?

   e. Did the vendor meet their commitments?

   f. Would they use that vendor again?

B. Financial Stability

1. Obtain a copy of the vendor's latest financial statement.

2. Check for the possibility of lawsuits pending against the vendor.

C. Maintenance Support

1. What is the guaranteed maintenance response time?

2. Where are back-up facilities located in case of a system breakdown?

3. How many service locations does the vendor have?

4. Where is the nearest parts depot located?

	VENDORS			
	1	2	3	4

5. What is the ratio of maintenance personnel to systems in your area? (A vendor with a small customer base may not be able to support the manpower and parts inventory needed to give you quick and adequate service.)

6. Is a maintenance contract available?

7. Does the maintenance contract include all parts and labor?

8. Is preventive maintenance performed?

D. Software Support

1. Does the vendor offer programming services, such as writing custom programs or modifying existing packages to fit your needs, updating implemented programs as required, etc.?

2. How long has the vendor had experience with the package programs they offer?

3. What is the ratio of programming staff to active installations? Is it adequate to program your system, as well as the vendor's other on-going installations?

4. What is the vendor's guaranteed software failure response time?

5. Does the vendor provide adequate operating manuals?

6. Does the vendor offer conversion assistance, and if so, at what cost?

	VENDORS			
	1	2	3	4

7. Does the vendor allow a complete system test prior to installation?

E. Training

1. Does the vendor offer free, unlimited training? If not, what is the hour limit and training charge thereafter?

2. How many people will the training include without an additional charge? What is the additional charge per person?

3. Will the vendor provide on-site training?

4. How many training personnel does the vendor have?

5. Does the vendor have an established training program, including materials?

6. Will you need new personnel to operate the computer, or can your present employees be trained?

II. HARDWARE

  A. List the hardware proposed.

  1. Central Processing Unit (CPU)

  2. Disc Storage

  3. Terminals (CRTs)

  4. Printers

  5. Other

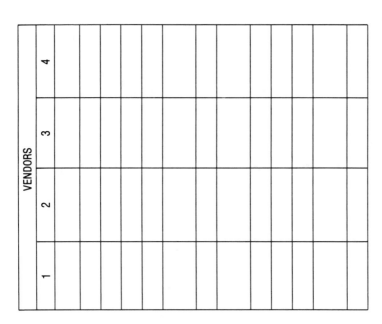

	VENDORS			
	1	2	3	4

B. List the expandable limits on the hardware proposed.
   1. CPU

   2. Disc Storage

   3. CRT's

   4. Printers

   5. Other

C. What are the facility requirements for the equipment (space, soundproofing, air conditioning, electrical capacity, etc.)?

D. When does the warranty expire?

III. SOFTWARE
A. What is the operating system used in the CPU?

B. How many jobs can the system handle simultaneously?

C. What language is the computer programmed in?

D. Does the vendor use software packages and/or provide custom programming?

E. Will the vendor modify their software packages to fit your current and changing needs?

F. How much modification is provided and at what cost to you?

	VENDORS			
	1	2	3	4
G. Does the vendor offer complete documentation of the system, including the following items?				
1. Systems Flowcharts				
2. File Layout Definitions				
3. Program Narratives				
H. Can the applications (such as inventory control, order entry and accounts receivable) be interrelated to eliminate duplicate entries?				
I. Does the software provide security levels?				
J. Do all the vendor's computers use the same software, or will you have to convert your software when you outgrow your current computer?				
K. Is there a warranty period, or will you be charged to eliminate bugs?				
L. Will you get a fixed quote on your software?				
M. Remember: Do not accept the computer until the software is completed to your specifications. Have all changes made before taking delivery. You should see your computer working "live" before you accept delivery.				

IV. PRICE

A. What is the hardware cost, including sales tax?

B. What is the software cost, including sales tax?

C. What are the costs for miscellaneous supplies, freight and insurance?

	VENDORS			
	1	2	3	4
D. What are the other costs, if any (such as facility requirements and personal property taxes)?				
E. What will be the total cost to deliver (items A, B, C and D above)?				
F. What is the annual maintenance cost for hardware?				
G. What is the annual maintenance cost for software?				
H. What will be the charge for training?				
I. Will it be necessary for you to hire additional personnel?				
J. What is the payment schedule?				
K. Remember: Be sure the vendor quotes all costs, such as hardware, software, supplies, training and maintenance, separately.				
V. GENERAL				
A. Does the vendor appear to understand your operational problems?				
B. Was the vendor prompt in his dealings with you? (This is often an indication regarding future service.)				
C. Were you comfortable in your dealings with this vendor?				
D. Did the proposal appear complete? Were any important items omitted?				
E. Is everything mentioned in the previous steps covered by the contract? (If you have a standard contract, the answer is "no.")				

7

How to Identify and Monitor the Key Financial Elements of Your Company

DURING MY PROFESSIONAL CAREER, I have seen companies in various industries—some with considerable sales volume—operating with systems that failed to give their owners or managers enough financial data to make effective business decisions. Far too often the end result of this lack of information and the overall system responsible for it lead to financial disaster. It is the management equivalent of anemia, and the results are sluggishness, lack of strength, wasted effort, and growing slovenliness.

Some responsible small business studies have demonstrated that a lack of adequate recordkeeping is a major cause of business failure. Nevertheless, I have seen and continue to see business people show little or no regard for the information necessary to manage their companies. I have heard accountants referred to as "a necessary evil," necessary only to help solve potential tax problems. I have seen people sell products without knowing what their costs are, and I've seen people bid jobs not based on whether they can make a profit for their company, but on the basis of what their competition is selling it for.

I have often wondered why this attitude regarding financial data is so prevalent. My conclusion is simple. Owners and managers of small companies find themselves in the position of leadership by accident rather than by design. They often lack the necessary knowledge to understand and utilize financial data.

Lack of experience leads them to conclude that financial data is for bankers, accountants, and the Internal Revenue Service, but not of much value in the decision making process.

THE BUCK STOPS WITH YOU

Every day huge amounts of activity take place within your company: invoices are written, orders taken, receivables collected, bills paid, bills incurred, loans are made or paid, inventory grows or shrinks, services are rendered, deposits made, production increases, production decreases, costs rise and occasionally fall, equipment is bought and sold, sales increase, sales decrease, people here, people there. Activity everywhere.

Overwhelming, isn't it? Yet, as the owner-manager of your company, you are responsible for monitoring, managing, and evaluating the results of all that activity. The buck stops with you.

WHAT'S THE BOTTOM LINE?

Does any of the following sound familiar? It was 9:00 a.m. on Thursday the 28th. The lights in our conference room beamed a warm glow over the table. Across the table from me was John Sloan. I handed John a copy of his quarterly report. His first words came quickly, "What's the bottom line?"

"A small profit," I reported.

"How much tax will I have to pay?"

"At this rate, not much," I answered.

"Good," John snapped back.

Today was going to be quite a day. Four meetings were scheduled, and all of them were for reviewing financial statements.

At 10:30 a.m., I met with Ron Agnew, the owner of a small

design company. Ron's opening words were, "How did we do tax-wise?"

Three hours later, I met with Sharon Samuelson, who had just started in business the previous year. A tall, rather slender woman, impeccably dressed, Sharon has great taste in clothes. Her taste has made her boutique quite successful.

When I handed Sharon her annual report, she looked at it and said, "Could you help me interpret this?" I smiled and proceeded to walk Sharon through the maze of accounting data. She was a good student but it was going to take more than one session to teach her how to use the information I had presented.

My last meeting of the day was with Eric Brown. You may remember Eric. His partner, Joe Scott, managed to take their company for an extra $250,000. When Joe left the company, all financial decisions fell to Eric. He was a fast learner. I presented him with his year-end report, but before he opened it, he fired a barrage of questions. "What's the bottom line? Will my banker be happy? How much tax do I have to pay? What I want is large profits to show the bank and no profits to show Uncle Sam!" Yes, Eric had learned fast. He knew the creed well. "Large profits to show the banker, and no profits for the Feds!"

Sounds familiar, doesn't it? The meetings were typical. Management not schooled in financial matters; always in a hurry, never taking the time to digest the results of operations and only interested in the "bottom line."

Yet, today's economic conditions demand that management of all companies, large or small, learn as much as possible about using and understanding financial accounting. Not too many years go, we could solve our financial problems by passing on price increases to our customers. That was accepted as part of the times. Inflation helped hide mistakes.

Today, however, inflation is gone, competition is tougher than ever, business is more complex, and money is harder to come by. It is far more important to master the skills necessary to keep our business alive. We must run our business in a business-like manner.

WHERE DO WE BEGIN?

First, we must learn to understand financial accounting. There are three ways to go about this:

Review the sample financial statement in Chapter 8 and follow the step-by-step comments.

Enroll in an accounting course for owners and managers of small businesses offered at your local university or college. This is the most time-consuming and will take some real dedication on your part.

The third method is the easiest and the least time consuming. Every time financial statements are prepared, have your accountant explain them in detail. Begin with this simple question, "Now that you've prepared this data, how is the information going to help me and my business?" At this point, he'll either panic because he doesn't understand the statements himself, or he'll proceed to explain their meaning.

Don't be embarrassed. If you don't understand him, ask questions; let him know you don't understand. He's schooled and trained in the meaning of financial statements; you're not! So don't be embarrassed to ask questions. If he's good, he'll take the time to explain the statements in a manner you can understand. If he can't explain them in a meaningful manner, seek help from someone who can.

HOW OFTEN?

Every business should review financial accounting once each month. This data should be compared to your budget on a line-by-line basis. If there is a problem getting the data monthly, have statements prepared no less than once each quarter.

In every case where I have seen a business person receiving monthly statements the comments have always been the same. "I don't know how I operated in the past without this information." I've heard that time and time again.

Many times, however, having an outside accounting firm prepare monthly statements can be expensive. The solution to the problem is simple. Have your accountants train your bookkeeping personnel to prepare the statements. Let the accountants confine their activity to a cursory review after the bookkeeper has completed the major portion of the work. This should reduce professional fees substantially and provide you with much-needed data.

If you don't have bookkeeping personnel, have your accountants recommend a competent free-lance bookkeeper. This service is considerably less expensive than using professional accountants to do your bookkeeping.

Remember, you are trying to develop a system to provide financial data regularly and to develop the skills necessary to interpret this data.

Understanding financial statements is not enough. You must have a management information system that monitors properly prepared financial statements, cash balances, future cash needs, accounts receivable and inventories.

CASH IS KING, ALWAYS HAS BEEN AND ALWAYS WILL BE.

Not too long ago, I met Bill Hall and Frieda Gunter. Bill started in the glass business many years ago. At that time, Frieda was his bookkeeper. Today, Frieda earns about $250,000 per year and owns 25 percent of the company.

Our first meeting went something like this: I entered the reception area of their business and waited for about five minutes. A young lady asked me to follow her. We proceeded to walk through a maze of hallways, making turns, entering offices, then returning to more hallways and more offices. We finally ended our journey in a conference room.

There sat Bill and Frieda, both in their mid-fifties. Bill had a dark complexion, was gray at the temples and a little on the pudgy side. Frieda was in her mid-fifties but looked close to sixty-five. We started our conversation with small talk and ultimately got around to the financial condition of the glass company. Theirs was a highly success-ful business generating large profits and very large amounts of cash. A cash cow!

Bill and Frieda's banker had referred us to them. "What a fine gentlemen Dave Reese (the banker) is," commented Frieda. "He takes us out to lunch at least once every other month and pays."

"What balances do you maintain in your accounts?" was my first question.

"We keep about eight-hundred in the checking account at all times."

"How do you manage to keep such a small float in the account?" I was obviously impressed with their cash management.

Frieda quickly corrected me, "Eight-hundred thousand."

"Eight-hundred thousand dollars in your checking account?" I quickly asked.

"Yes," Frieda beamed.

After I regained my composure, I managed to squeak out an "oh" without being too emotional. Now I understand why the banker took them to lunch so often. He was a real sport.

"Frieda, do you know you could be earning an extra $100,000 to $150,000 per year on your money if you moved it to some kind of money market instrument?" I asked. She smiled but said nothing.

Ultimately they became clients of our firm. The first thing we did was to fill out the forms for a money market account. It took Frieda almost six weeks to sign them and transfer the funds. I was annoyed not only with Frieda's attitude, throwing away $100,000 to $150,000, but I was also angry with her banker who was doing absolutely nothing to help his customer. Why they never changed to another bank is beyond me. Incidentally, Frieda left the company when Bill concluded that $250,000 a year was too much to pay for a bookkeeper.

CASH COSTS MONEY!

Cash is one of the most expensive commodities we use in running our businesses. Think about it for a moment. In many businesses, other than cost of sales, and hopefully your salary, the cost of cash (interest) is one of the largest expense items a company has.

MANAGE CASH MORE EFFECTIVELY

Ask your bookkeeper to grab a sheet of paper and title it "Cash Flow from _____ to _____" (use only a 15-day period, *i.e.*, from 1/1 to 1/15).

A. Cash at the beginning of the period _____

B. Estimated collections for the period _____

C. Borrowings anticipated for the period _____

D. Total cash available _____

E. Bills to be paid (subtract) (_____)

F. Loan payments to be made (subtract) (_____)

G. Payroll and payroll taxes (subtract) (_____)

H. Ending cash for the period (subtract lines E, F, and G from line D) _____

After doing the above, at least you know where you will be in the next two weeks. This will give you a very short-term cash projection and allow you to manage your float more effectively. Ideally you should have this kind of projection for at least six months to one year in advance. This will give you the ability to arrange your future cash needs well in advance.

THE ONE-YEAR CASH FORECAST

Once your profit and loss budget is completed, it is necessary to convert the profit and loss numbers to a cash flow forecast. Cash forecasting is more difficult to do, but it is necessary to have some idea of future cash needs. The following cash forecast follows the budget outlined in Chapter 4.

STEP 1—GET HELP

Find someone in your organization to work with you in completing the details. This will relieve you from a highly laborious task.

STEP 2—MAKE ASSUMPTIONS

The key to reasonably accurate cash flow forecasting is the assumptions that are used in the forecasting preparation. Here is a list of areas where assumptions must be made to provide accuracy in your forecast.

CASH COLLECTIONS

Generally, there are four alternative methods that can be used to determine how cash is going to be collected. Use the alternative you feel most comfortable with.

Alternative 1. If you are in a 100 percent cash-and-carry business— all sales are collected in the month the sales are made.

Alternative 2. Be arbitrary. Guess what you believe the collections will be during each month of the year. This method, while not very accurate, is often used.

Alternative 3. Is similar to the second method used with sales forecasting in your profit and loss budget preparation. You would assume, as in the example, total sales are going to be $1,870,000 for the year, and you may further assume that they will be 80 percent collected during the year. This gives you total cash collections of $1,496,000 ($1,870,000 x .80). Go back to prior years to see what each month's relationship of collections is to the year's total. Apply that percentage to the total annual collections you expect to receive.

Example:

Prior Year's Collection		% of Total Collection		*Expected Collection	Monthly Collection
Jan	$ 137,000	9.3	X	1,496,000 = $	139,128
Feb	130,000	8.8	X	1,496,000 =	131,648
March	135,000	9.1	X	1,496,000 =	136,136
April	160,000	10.8	X	1,496,000 =	161,568
May	140,000	9.6	X	1,496,000 =	143,616
June	120,000	8.1	X	1,496,000 =	121,176
July	120,000	8.1	X	1,496,000 =	121,176
Aug	100,000	6.8	X	1,496,000 =	101,728
Sept	110,000	7.4	X	1,496,000 =	110,704
Oct	110,000	7.4	X	1,496,000 =	110,704
Nov	100,000	6.8	X	1,496,000 =	101,728
Dec	115,000	7.8	X	1,496,000 =	116,688
Total	$ 1,477,000	100.0			$ 1,496,000

*Total sales $1,870,000—assume collecting 80% during year = $1,496,000

Alternative 4. Assume that a month's sales will be converted to cash consistently in the months following the month of the sale. For example, in our budget, we have indicated that $129,000 of sales will be made in the month of January. Look at history or just make arbitrary assumptions that those sales will be collected, let's say, 45 percent in the month of the sale, 40 percent in the first month following the sale, and 15 percent in the second month following the sale. We can then forecast our cash collections using this method for each month throughout the year.

YOUR COMPANY, INC.
CASH COLLECTION
ON THE YEAR

	Jan.	Feb.	Mar.	Apr.	May
Sales	129,030	129,030	129,030	129,030	192,610
Previous Months					
December Previous Years	20,000	10,000			
Collection Current Year					
Jan. 129,030 x 45;40;15	58,063	51,612	19,355		
Feb. 129,030 x 45;40;15		58,063	51,612	19,355	
Mar. 129,030 x 45;40;15			58,063	51,612	19,355
Apr. 129,030 x 45;40;15				58,063	51,612
May 192,610 x 45;40;15					86,675
Jun. 192,610 x 45;40;15					
Jul. 162,690 x 45;40;15					
Aug. 129,030 x 45;40;15					
Sep. 192,610 x 45;40;15					
Oct. 129,610 x 45;40;15					
Nov. 162,690 x 45;40;15					
Dec. 192,610 x 45;40;15					
Total Collections	78,063	119,675	129,030	129,030	157,642

The assumption used for cash collection
is that:
45% of the months sales are collected in the
month the sale is made.

40% of the sale is collected in the 1st
month following the sale

15% is collected in the 2nd month
following the sale
    in otherwords   45; 40; 15

Jun.	Jul.	Aug.	Sep.	Oct.	Nov.	Dec.	Total
192,610	162,690	129,030	192,610	129,030	162,690	192,610	1,870,000
							30,000
							129,030
							129,030
							129,030
19,355							129,030
77,044	28,891						192,610
86,675	77,044	28,891					192,610
	73,210	65,076	24,404				162,690
		58,063	51,612	19,355			129,030
			86,675	77,044	28,891		192,610
				58,063	51,612	19,355	129,030
					73,210	65,076	138,286
						86,674	86,674
183,074	179,145	152,030	162,691	154,462	153,713	171,105	1,769,660

PAYMENT OF EXPENSES

Here are four methods to help you determine how bills will be paid:

Alternative 1. Assume that all expenses are paid during the month they are incurred. This will simplify the cash forecasting process, but it isn't very realistic. There aren't too many businesses paying all of their bills each month.

Alternative 2. Take a look at each expense item on the profit and loss budget, then decide when that expense will be paid. For example, when you look at rent, you know you generally pay it each month. When you look at office supplies, it may be that you pay them in the month following the incurrence of the expense. Or it is even possible that you are on a 60- or 90-day basis after you incur the expense. Attempt to match each expense to the actual month in which it will more than likely be paid.

Alternative 3. Assume a certain percentage of the bills incurred each month will be paid during the month incurred, a percentage in the first month following that month, and a percentage in the second month following the month incurred. This is exactly the method used in Alternative 4 for cash collections.

Alternative 4. To add more precision to Alternative 3, you could actually take your total expenses for a given month, subtract all those payments that you know will be paid during the month incurred, and then compute the balance left in the manner indicated in Alternative 3.

OTHER RECEIPTS

When doing your cash forecasting, it is necessary to assume the inflow of any additional funds that come either from investors, bank loans, sale of assets, or any other source. It is important to know when these amounts will be received to apply them to your projection for the proper month.

ADDITIONAL PAYMENTS

Not only is it necessary to forecast the payment of expenses, but it is also necessary to include in your forecast any additional cash being disbursed for deposits, purchase of assets, down payment on the purchase of assets, principal payments on loans outstanding, payment for deposits of income taxes, payroll taxes, and any other cash outflow you feel will be incurred during the period you are forecasting.

WORDS OF CAUTION

I have simplified the steps for preparing a cash forecast and the profit and loss budget. It is necessary that *all* businesses do some kind of budgeting and cash forecasting.

As your business gets larger and as it becomes more complex with unusual cash transactions, different kinds of expenses, the desire to maintain certain inventory levels, the receiving of customer deposits, and a myriad of other complex cash transactions, it will be necessary for you to become more precise in your forecasting and budgets.

When your business is at that stage of development, you may want to seek professional help either from within the company (hire personnel with the capability of doing more complex financial forecasting) or from outside the company. It is a must.

YOUR COMPANY, INC.
PAYMENT OF BILLS

	Jan.	Feb.	Mar.	Apr.	May
Total Expenses					
Cost of Goods Sold	58,063	58,063	58,063	58,063	86,675
Bills Paid	72,619	72,619	72,619	72,619	80,484
Total to be paid	130,682	130,682	130,682	130,682	167,159
Regular Payments:					
Interest	3,125	3,125	3,125	3,125	4,375
Legal and Accounting	1,000	1,000	1,000	1,000	1,000
Rent	4,000	4,000	4,000	4,000	4,000
Salaries	21,000	21,000	21,000	21,000	21,000
Taxes/payroll	4,200	4,200	4,200	4,200	4,200
Telephone	2,750	2,750	2,750	2,750	2,750
Total regular payments	36,075	36,075	36,075	36,075	37,325
Non-regular payments	94,607	94,607	94,607	94,607	129,834
Previous month December	65,000	10,000			
Regular Payments	36,075	36,075	36,075	36,075	37,325
Jan: 94,607 x 80;20		75,686	18,921		
Feb: 94,607 x 80;20			75,686	18,921	
Mar: 94,607 x 80;20				75,686	18,921
Apr: 94,607 x 80;20					75,686
May: 129,834 x 80;20					
Jun: 129,834 x 80;20					
Jul: 113,220 x 80;20					
Aug: 94,607 x 80;20					
Sep: 129,834 x 80;20					
Oct: 94,607 x 80;20					
Nov: 113,220 x 80;20					
Dec: 130,472 x 80;20					
Bills paid	101,075	121,761	130,682	130,682	131,932
Less depreciation expense, which is a non-paid expenditure	(7,000)	(7,000)	(7,000)	(7,000)	(7,000)
Bills paid	94,075	114,761	123,682	123,682	124,932

assumption for the payment of bills is; the
Total amounts to be paid less the amounts
regularly paid each month equals the non-
regular payments. These non-regular
Payments will be paid 80% in the month
following the month incurred – 20% in the
month following that. Thus 80:20

Jun.	Jul.	Aug.	Sep.	Oct.	Nov.	Dec.	TOTAL
86,675	73,211	58,063	86,675	58,063	73,211	86,675	841,500
80,484	81,933	78,543	85,158	78,543	82,008	85,796	943,425
167,159	155,144	136,606	171,833	136,606	155,219	172,471	1,784,925
4,375	4,375	4,450	4,450	4,450	4,450	4,450	47,875
1,000	1,000	1,000	1,000	1,000	1,000	1,000	12,000
4,000	4,000	4,000	4,000	4,000	4,000	4,000	48,000
21,000	24,833	24,833	24,833	24,833	24,833	24,833	275,000
4,200	4,966	4,966	4,966	4,966	4,966	4,966	55,000
2,750	2,750	2,750	2,750	2,750	2,750	2,750	33,000
37,325	41,924	41,999	41,999	41,999	41,999	41,999	470,875
129,834	113,220	94,607	129,834	94,607	113,220	130,472	1,314,050
							75,000
37,325	41,924	41,999	41,999	41,999	41,999	41,999	470,875
							94,607
							94,607
							94,607
18,921							94,607
103,867	25,967						129,834
	103,867	25,967					129,834
		90,576	22,644				113,220
			75,686	18,921			94,607
				103,867	25,967		129,834
					75,686	18,921	94,607
						104,377	104,377
160,113	171,758	158,542	140,329	164,787	143,652	165,297	1,720,610
(7,000)	(7,000)	(7,000)	(7,000)	(7,000)	(7,000)	(7,000)	(84,000)
153,113	164,758	151,542	133,329	157,787	136,652	158,297	1,636,610

YOUR COMPANY, INC.
CASH FORECAST

see page 78-79
See page 82-83

		Jan.	Feb.	Mar.	Apr.	May
Total Collections		78,063	119,675	129,030	129,030	157,642
Less Bills Paid		94,075	114,761	123,682	123,682	124,932
Cash From Operations		(16,012)	4,914	5,348	5,348	32,710
Other Cash Payments:						
Purchase of Equipment						
Equipment—March						
Cost	150,000					
Finance	100,000					
Cash	50,000			(50,000)		
Automobile—July						
Cost	18,000					
Finance	(12,000)					
Cash	6,000					
Principle Payments on Financing*						
100,000 for 60 months						(1,666)
6,000 for 36 months						
Cash Flow for Period		(16,012)	4,914	(44,652)	5,348	31,044
Cash on Hand at						
Beginning of Period		36,000	19,988	24,902	(19,750)	(14,402)
Cash Balance at						
End of Period		19,988	24,902	(19,750)	(14,402)	16,642

*Principle payments only—interest is included in expense.

It appears as though some short term borrowing will be necessary to offset this obvious cash crunch

Jun.	Jul.	Aug.	Sep.	Oct.	Nov.	Dec.	Total
183,074	179,145	152,030	162,691	154,462	153,713	171,105	1,769,660
153,113	164,758	151,542	133,329	157,787	136,652	158,297	1,636,610
29,961	14,387	488	29,362	(3,325)	17,061	12,808	133,050
							(50,000)
	(6,000)						(6,000)
(1,666)	(1,666)	(1,666)	(1,666)	(1,666)	(1,666)	(1,666)	(13,328)
		(167)	(167)	(167)	(167)	(167)	(835)
28,295	6,721	(1,345)	27,529	(5,158)	15,228	10,975	62,887
16,642	44,937	51,658	50,313	77,842	72,684	87,912	36,000
44,937	51,658	50,313	77,842	72,684	87,912	98,887	99,467

MAKE YOUR CHECKING ACCOUNT OBSOLETE

Try to deposit all daily receipts directly to a money market account rather than into your checking account. Transfer funds from the money market account to a checking account only when you anticipate writing checks. Confine checkwriting to once or twice per month to allow the float in the money market account to build and earn additional interest.

Don't get caught up by the notion that your banker will treat you better if you keep high balances in a checking account. He may like you better, but you should earn as much as you can on your money. Today the banking business is far more competitive than it's ever been. If you are a good customer of your bank, you can have a lot of influence with your banker. But always keep another bank in reserve, just in case.

REDUCE THE RENT ON YOUR CASH

Sounds silly doesn't it? Yet, we do rent the use of money. Therefore, our goal should be to reduce the rent.

The banking industry is extremely competitive, which means more favorable credit terms. Ask your accountant to help you select a bank and banker. Accountants and bankers have mutual referral network which can be of value to you.

BANKERS HAVE PROBLEMS TOO!

Jane Cole started our phone conversation with an angry comment. "The financial statement you sent us was wrong."

"Jane, we never sent you a financial statement and we haven't even done any work on your account," I responded.

"Well, I sent what you gave me to the bank and we got our loan, but the statement was wrong," Jane claimed.

"I don't know what you sent but it obviously worked. Why don't you get a copy of the statement and read it to me and let's see if I can figure out what you did," I said.

Ten minutes later Jane called back.

"The name of the company is XYZ, Inc. and all the dates have 19xx," she said.

"Jane, you sent the bank a sample promotional statement we provide new clients. It is meaningless. It's a nonexistent company. It does say a lot about your banker, doesn't it?" We both laughed.

If you're using a lender other than a bank or thrift and loan, you're more than likely paying interest in excess of what a bank or thrift would charge. I refer to these lenders as second-level financing companies. They usually base their loans on underlying collateral you've supplied as security for the loan, and they charge handsomely for the money. The goal is to improve the financial position of *your* company, not theirs. You need to become bankable as quickly as possible. To do this, you have to become more profitable, improve your cash flow, and operate your business in a business-like manner. You almost have to put yourself in a position where you don't need the money, then they'll be happy to loan it to you.

GET MORE MONEY BY BEING PREPARED

Here are some tips on how to be prepared:

- Have your accountant introduce you to a banker. He will have access to high levels in the bank that you might not otherwise have. Don't just walk in off the street.

- Bring current financial statements consisting of a Balance Sheet, a Profit and Loss Statement, a Statement of Changes in Financial Position and footnote disclosures. The bank may require these statements to be "Reviewed" or "Audited" by a CPA.

- Bankers will want to review your history so be prepared to present two or three years' prior financial statements and/or tax returns.

- Generally, you will personally guarantee the business loan so have your personal financial statements and tax returns available.

- Bring financial forecasts. This will consist of projected profit and loss and cash-flow statements for at least one year in advance. It will also show the banker that you are sophisticated in your management approach.
- Provide a breakdown of what you're going to use the money for.
- Prepare a packet of additional information which might consist of brochures, sales literature, contracts, history of the company, publicity, research projects, etc. Gather all the propaganda you can muster to show the banker that you are someone they must do business with.
- Watch your appearance. First impressions are lasting.

IT'S 10:00 P.M.

Do you know where your cash is? If it's not in your pocket, it's more than likely in accounts receivable and/or inventory—two items that sop up your cash like a slice of rye in a bowl of chicken soup.

THEY JUST GET LARGER AND LARGER

Do you remember the old joke about "The Three Famous Lies"? One of the lies was "the check is in the mail."

Now when you call a customer for payment they never say the check is in the mail, they say, "the check is being cut, but first we need a copy of the invoice. We seem to have misplaced it." Does that sound familiar? (You wouldn't be doing that yourself now, would you?) They have just borrowed your money for 25 additional days, interest-free. Five days to send the invoice copy, five days in their accounting department for approval, five days for "cutting the check," five days for signature, then five more days back in the mail.

Accounts receivable (amounts people owe you) is probably the fastest growing asset in your company. The balance just seems to get larger and larger and larger. Remember, cash is king and we have to get our hands on as much as possible. Therefore, monitoring and collecting accounts receivable is one of our most important functions.

BE SYSTEMATIC IN YOUR APPROACH TO COLLECTIONS

Here are some tips on speeding up the collection of your accounts receivable.

- Sit down with your bookkeeper every two weeks and review a listing of the accounts receivable.

- Call delinqent customers immediately.

- Have nasty letters sent to slow pays. Three is sufficient, and they should generally follow this order: The first letter should ask for payment and give approximately 20 days for results. The second letter, which is sent out after the 20 days, should be a threat to turn the matter over to your attorney for collection. Give them about 10 more days. The third letter which goes out after the 10 days, should say the account is going to be turned over for collection within 48 hours. If you don't get any results within the 48 hours, turn it over for collection.

- These letters should be computer printouts, if possible. If you send a letter to a long-time customer and he calls and says, "Listen you son-of-a-bitch, I've been dealing with you for years and now you send me one of those letters. I'm pissed." Your quick response should be, "Oh my god, our computer screwed up. It's a computer error!" Then gently ask for payment.

- Monitor the total receivable balances daily.

- When you are instructing someone in your organization on the procedures for collecting the accounts receivable, be specific, give names and phone numbers to call and amounts you'd like to see collected.

- Charge interest or service charges on old balances.

- If you can't get paid in full, ask for partial payment.

- If you are not being paid regularly, your invoice may be going through the bookkeeping department with little concern on their part, to pay the bill. Send a copy of the invoice to your contact at the company with a note to "please take care of this." You may get faster results. Often times your contact may not realize your bill is not being paid.

- After your credit manager or bookkeeper has called several times, the debtor knows exactly why they are calling and will ignore the call. Have the bookkeeper leave a new name.... Bridget is a good one. There isn't a businessman alive who would not return a call from a Bridget. For those of you who are dealing with women customers, Lance might suffice. If Bridget calls, watch out! She may be dunning you.

- Here is a familiar scenario: You instruct your bookkeeper to call on all accounts past due. She starts at the top of the list at the letter "A", gets interrupted, starts over at A. She gets interrupted again, and starts back at A. Another interruption and back to, you guessed it, "A". Once in awhile have the bookkeeper work up the list starting with "Z"

- Put past due accounts on a cash and carry basis.

- Check your customer's current financial condition. They may be having worse problems than you.

- Bug the hell out of them.

- If all else fails, sue the bastard.

By monitoring your accounts receivable daily and becoming tough with the debtor, additional cash will be squeezed out of those accounts receivable balances. Cash is king.

THE FANTASY ASSET

I like to refer to inventory as the "fantasy asset." More games are played and guesses are made on the value shown as inventory on financial statements than any other item in the statement. This occurs so often that many times management loses sight of the importance of proper control and evaluation of inventory—the single most important asset in determining company profitability. Yet the fantasy goes on. Need more profit? Up the inventory. Pay lower taxes? Lower the inventory. Take an inventory? Too much trouble. Price it right? Too much detail. What's the inventory? Nobody knows. "Plug a number," so the saying goes.

If you use an incorrect inventory for your financial statement, your profit or loss statement will be incorrect by the same amount on a dollar-for-dollar ratio. Yet, guesses are made and the fantasy goes on and on and on.

A RULE TO REMEMBER

The profit and loss statement is absolutely worthless unless an accurately counted and priced (valued) inventory is used in the statement. You'll never know the true profit if the fantasy prevails; you're only fooling yourself.

FANTASY STORIES

Dave, Glenda, and Al Marcus sat quietly as I handed them their company's year-end statement. They were running a family business that was growing by leaps and bounds. Cash balances were running lower than their expectations, and they were concerned as to whether or not they were making a profit.

Dave began, "Are we on the right track? Are we making a profit?"

"Dave, I must be frank with you. The statement shows a profit, but as you know, much of the inventory was what you called an 'educated guess.' If the number you gave us is right, then yes, there is a profit. However, there are no cost records of your work-in-process inventory and no material and labor costs for work completed. So to answer your question directly, I don't know. What you need is a cost system that will tell you the material, labor, and overhead on each job and reflect accurate inventory value. This is a must for your business."

Dave responded quickly, "Maybe later."

Jim Williams is a man in his late fifties. He and his son were running a company that manufactured toilets.

"Jim what does it cost you to manufacture a toilet?" I asked.

"I don't know" was his response.

"How do you know what to sell it for?" I asked.

"We've been selling it at that price for years" was his last comment.

Bill Bennet and his partner Harold Mahler thought they were very clever. They got into the business of manufacturing household products out of wood. Items such as breadboxes, saltshakers, canisters, etc. Sales were almost $12 million. You may have purchased one yourself; their products were well made, and they were everywhere.

One day in a meeting we were discussing the financial statement of the company. I urged them to hire a controller. Harold's father, Sam, was doing the books, and he was incompetent. You couldn't rely on anything he gave you. I also was bugging them to get a cost accounting system installed to ascertain proper inventory costs. They were manufacturing a multitude of different products, but there wasn't one piece of paper available to indicate what the product cost.

"Harold, you've got to get rid of Sam and bring in a controller and a cost accountant. The business is growing; you can no longer operate as a 'mom and pop organization.'"

"I know, but how can I fire my Dad?" Harold asked.

"That's a tough one, but you need a better controller."

"Maybe later," was Harold's cool reply. "By the way, I've installed a cost accounting system."

"Huh, when did you do that?"

"Not too long ago. We measure the trash in the barrels."

"What?"

"Every night we go to the waste bins and measure our scrap lumber. This gives us a method of measuring costs. Too much scrap, too much cost."

Needless to say, I was amazed. I had never heard of such a thing before.

Steve Jenkins was great with the fantasy asset. His company was losing its shirt yet the financial statements indicated a profit. He was in the underwear business. Obviously, the company was losing its undershirt. After he left the company, we found out the games he was playing. At the end of every year he would change his computer to up the value of his inventory so that he would show a profit.

Eventually Steve sold out to one of his employees. This has always puzzled me. The employees knew what Steve was doing yet bought the business based on this fantasy inventory and phony financial statements.

Steve was last heard from somewhere in Arizona. The company, after 42 years in business, went into bankruptcy.

By the way, Jim Williams' toilet business died a slow death. Dave Marcus' company is installing a cost system and doing well, and Harold fired his father just prior to a major creditor closing them down.

THERE ARE NO EASY SOLUTIONS

Inventory control is the most difficult area in running a business yet the most vital. There are no easy solutions to inventory control, but I do have some practical suggestions:

- Use perpetual inventory records for the large dollar amounts of inventory. You don't have to maintain records on the entire inventory. Usually 20 percent of the inventory items accounts for 80 percent of the dollars. Maintain records on 20 percent of the items that account for the 80 percent of the dollars and not on the 80 percent of the items that account for 20 percent of the dollars.

- Take physical inventories regularly and compare the physical inventory with your perpetual records to test the perpetual records for accuracy.

- If taking a physical inventory is a large task, take counts on a cycle. This may mean counting a fourth of the inventory every three months or a sixth every two months.

- The small and low value items should not be included in your routine inventory counts. Count them once or twice a year; use your judgement.

- If the physical inventories and the perpetual inventory are in agreement, the perpetual inventories can be used for financial accounting.

- All differences between the physical inventory and the perpetual inventory should be reconciled.

- As soon as an item in inventory appears to be slow moving, reduce the price and get rid of it. This will keep your inventory fresh at all times.

- If you manufacture a product, a cost accounting system that determines the cost of your product should be developed. This will aid in the determination of the price your product will be sold for.

- Sell your product by calculating the sales price in the following manner:

Material cost   _____
Labor cost   _____
Factory overhead   _____
Selling costs   _____
Administrative costs   _____
Profit   _____
Total sales price   _____

- Don't be foolish when working with your inventory in determining costs and/or systems. If you are in doubt about what you are doing, seek professional advice.

- If you are in the construction business, whether you're building buildings or painting walls, develop job-cost accounting. This will allow you to keep track of materials and labor on all jobs, and it will be of great assistance in determining productivity, bidding procedures, and pinning down where you've made mistakes.

- Adopt and maintain written policies and procedures to implement all inventory procedures.
- Automate, automate, automate. (see Chapter 6.)
- Review inventory reports and procedures regularly.
- Stop fantasizing.

TAKE AN ACCURATE INVENTORY

Good housekeeping is an important factor in taking a physical inventory. Your inventory can be taken more quickly and more accurately if you begin with the following steps:

- Move identical goods to the same location.
- Place inventory in order.
- Make all items readily identifiable.
- Clear aisles and passageways.
- Segregate scrap and worthless items.

If your business is a manufacturing entity, schedule production so that work-in-process is kept to a minimum. This will reduce the time and effort required to count and price those items.

INVENTORY INSTRUCTIONS

Management should prepare detailed instructions for taking the inventory. These instructions should include cut-off procedures for shipping and receiving departments, complete procedures for counting the inventory, and the name of the individual to contact if there are questions. All participants should attend a meeting to review the instructions.

ESTABLISHING THE CUT-OFF

A proper cut-off involves identifying the arrival and shipment dates of your inventory. This is essential because it defines the items to be included in your inventory. Under ideal circumstances all activities in the shipping and receiving departments would be stopped; however, many times this is not possible.

Goods received after the cut-off date should be physically segregated and counted separately. The receiving documents should indicate the date the shipment was received. This will facilitate the accounting of the related invoices. If the items are shipped during the inventory, the shipment date should be noted on the shipping records. This will identify the last invoices to be included in the current accounting period.

COUNTING THE INVENTORY

Thorough planning will help eliminate problems that can occur in counting inventory. Your planning should cover topics such as inventory counting teams, the layout of the warehouse, pre-numbered inventory count tags, and supervision.

- The counting teams should consist of two individuals: one as a counter and the other as a recorder. These individuals should be familiar with the items to be counted but, if possible, should not be employees who work in the warehouse. Employees who have regular access to the inventory may be able to hide any defalcation by falsifying counts.

- Each counting team should be assigned an area of the warehouse. Those sections should be easily distinguishable from each other. For example, aisles may be used as boundaries. This will decrease the possibility of inventory being counted twice, thus creating false profits.

- Once the counting teams have been assigned their areas, pre-numbered inventory tags should be distributed to them. When filled in, the tags will contain a description of the item, the quantity of items counted, the units in which they were counted (for example, one dozen each), an identification of the inventory counting team, and test-count information.

- As the tags are issued, the supervisor should maintain a control sheet showing which tags were distributed to which teams. For

example, tags 1 through 100 might be given to counting team A,
and 101 to 150 to team B.

- All items of inventory should be tagged. After the counts have
  been made, a tour of the areas to see that all items have been
  tagged is appropriate. After this is complete, then all tags should
  be pulled.

- The completed tags will be placed in the inventory areas in boxes
  or on shelves. The supervisor will subsequently collect the tags,
  place them in numerical sequence again, and tabulate the results.
  Unused tags will be returned to the supervisor to ensure all tags
  have been accounted for. If your inventory tags are not pre-
  numbered and some are misplaced, your final figures will be
  inaccurate. Prenumbering the tags is designed to eliminate that
  possibility.

- To count large quantities more efficiently, consider the following shortcuts: You can use a scale to determine quantity. For
  example, if you know that 100 bolts weigh approximately 4
  ounces, you can calculate the total number of bolts by weighing
  them. You can also precount portions of the material prior to the
  formal inventory. In this way, in the weeks preceding the actual
  inventory, employees can use their "spare time" to count some
  of the items. If precounting is used, be sure a precount slip is
  attached to each container, showing the quantity and description
  of the item, as well as the initials of the employee and the date of
  the count. The containers should then be sealed. If any of the
  units are removed from a precounted container, it must be indicated on the precount slip.

- Adequate supervision is a must. It provides the assurance that all
  procedures are being followed as prescribed by management.
  The supervisor can solve problems that arise, such as identifying
  unusual goods, and should conduct random checks of some of
  the sections that have been counted.

The secret to a successful inventory is careful planning.
These guidelines should make your inventory more accurate
and more efficient and prevent the complications typically associated with this procedure.

THESE POINTS CANNOT BE OVEREMPHASIZED

Management must monitor cash and accounts receivable daily. Know what your commitments are, work the cash, and work the accounts receivable. With today's high interest rates, cash management will mean the difference between success and failure. Cash is king, queen, prince, and all other titles of royalty. It is our blood.

Cost accounting and inventory controls are absolutely necessary where appropriate in your business. You will never be able to know whether your business is profitable or not without accurate physical counts and proper pricing of your inventories.

Monitor financial statements every month. These financial statements should be compared to previously established targets and goals. This will enable you to monitor the financial results of the decisions you've made and to know whether you are achieving your goals.

As an owner-manager of a business, you must keep your finger on the pulse of all phases of the operation. Set in motion a management information system that gives you a constant flow of information regarding your company's financial position and the efficiency of operations at all levels. Regularly monitor sales, accounts receivable, cash balances, and budgets. You will not compile this type of information. Do not bog yourself down in details. Monitor and review the information, then distribute it to subordinates and suggest corrective action.

8
What Do
All the
Numbers Mean?

FINANCIAL STATEMENTS are a summary of all financial transactions that have taken place within the company. Before an
analysis of the financial statements can be made, you must have a
basic understanding of the terminology used. The following list
details the most widely used terms in financial statements. This list
corresponds to the items listed on the financial statement at the end
of this chapter. Make a photo-copy and check against the various
categories as you read through the terms and their applications.

(A) The Balance Sheet is a statement of the assets, liabilities, and net
worth of the company at any given time.

1. *Current assets* are assets which will generally convert to cash within 12 months.

2. *Property and equipment* are assets that have a useful life to the
   business for a substantial period of time and which are amortized
   (or depreciated) over this useful life.

3. *Other assets* are assets that cannot be listed in categories (1) and
   (2). They are often not liquid and are held for some purpose
   other than the general operation of the business. This may
   include purchased goodwill, securities held for investments, etc.

4. *Current liabilities* are those liabilities which are expected to be paid
   within 12 months or within the operating cycle of the business.

5. *Long-term debt* comprises liabilities which are due to mature beyond 12 months. Twelve-month maturities are in the current liability section.

6. *Stockholders' equity* is the book value, or book equity, of a corporation. It consists of the original investment and subsequent investments of the shareholders plus the net earnings retained in the business. The stockholders' equity is reduced by any dividends paid.

7. In an unincorporated business, this section is called *Proprietors Equity*. This is the money the owners have put into the business plus profits remaining in the business, less any funds taken by the owners and less any losses of the business.

(B) Statement of Income is the statement that shows the final results of all the revenue and expense transactions of the business. They either produce income or a loss.

1. *Sales* is generally the first item on the income statement indicating the net sales of the company for the period indicated.

2. *Cost of goods sold* is the direct cost of the items sold during the period. In a manufacturing business, this would include direct materials, labor, and overhead.

3. *Gross profit* is the profit before operating expenses of the business. Gross profit is the result of sales minus the cost of goods sold. This is often called the gross margin.

4. *Selling and administrative expenses* are the operating expenses of the business.

5. *Income before officers' compensation* is the income before any compensation is paid to officers. Many companies like to have this number shown on the income statement so that they can explain to bankers and other users of the statements what the income of the business is before the owners or officers have compensated themselves. This is more cosmetic than substantive.

6. *Compensation paid to officers* is shown separately to display to the

users the amount of monies being taken by officers and often times, owners.

7. *Income before provision for income tax* is the pretax earnings of the business. Proprietorships and partnerships do not have this item on their income statement. The proprietors and/or partners report their share of the income on their personal tax returns, and their tax expense is not that of the business.

8. *Net income* is the "bottom line." This is the profit or loss of the business.

(C) Statement of Changes in Financial Position is the statement that reflects the changes of the financial position of the company between periods. Often this statement is presented by showing the changes in the working capital of the company. Most accountants prepare this statement because it is easy to prepare. Another method of showing the changes in the financial position of the company is to show the actual changes in the cash position of the company. The statement of changes in financial position reflecting the changes in cash is the most useful method in preparing the statement. Generally, management wants to know where the cash came from and where it went. This statement provides the answers.

The following list is of the major items on the Statement of Changes with a brief explanation of each:

1. *Source of cash* will list all the sources of cash available to the business for the period indicated in the statement.

2. *Net income* in the source of cash section will be adjusted to reflect the actual cash that was provided by the operation of the business. Therefore, the statement generally starts with the net income and adjusts the net income for any noncash items. This is illustrated in item 3, below, depreciation.

3. *Depreciation* is an expense of the business that did not require the outlay of cash. Therefore, it is added to net income.

4. *Other items* affecting cash from operations would include a list of all of the various items that must be added to or subtracted from

net income to compute the actual cash that was provided from operations. For example, during the period of the statement, the accounts receivable decreased by $1,179. A decrease in accounts receivable means that the cash collected from accounts receivable was greater than the additional accounts receivable. This gives rise to a cash increase of $1,179 in our example. This is why $1,179 is added to the net income to derive the cash that was provided from the operations of the business.

The increase in inventory as illustrated in the example is $14,280. As we all know, an increase in inventory results in a shrinkage in cash from the operation of the business, therefore, this item is being subtracted from net income.

Increase in prepaid expenses also results in a reduction of cash used during the operation of the business.

Increase in accounts payable as illustrated is $53,108. To adjust the net income to the actual cash provided by the operations of the business, you must treat any increase in accounts payable as if it had been additional borrowings by the company. Therefore, it increases the amount of cash during the operation of the business. In the illustration, $53,108 of additional funds was made available by suppliers. Accordingly, add this to net income. The other items listed under section 4 have similar explanations.

5. *Cash provided by operations* is the actual cash that the operations of the business brought to the business.

    In the illustration, additional cash was provided by an officer who decreased loans that he owed to the company.

6. *Total cash provided* is the total cash that became available to the business for the period indicated in the Statement of Changes in Financial Position.

7. *Uses of cash* is the section that shows exactly what management did with the cash they had available during the period. As indicated, management purchased plant machinery and equip-

ment, paid down a significant amount on debt, and increased cash value of officers' life insurance.

8. *Total cash used* is the total of the cash spent during the period on other than operations of the business. Increase in cash during the period is $52,453. This is derived by taking the cash provided—$159,116 minus $106,663 cash used—resulting in an increase in cash of $52,453.

9. *Cash-beginning of the year* is the cash the company started with. If you add the cash that was generated during the period to the beginning cash, the result is item 12, which is cash at the end of the period.

(D) Schedule of Selling and Administrative Expenses illustrates the details of the items that make up the total selling expenses and the administrative expenses for the period.

USING RATIOS TO INTERPRET THE DATA

The financial statement alone will give some indication of the company's health but to see beyond the raw data, greater analysis is necessary. Most accountants and users of financial statements use ratio analysis. This is an excellent tool to determine the health of the company and whether management has made good use of company resources.

The following is a ratio analysis of the financial statements appearing at the end of this chapter.

CURRENT RATIO:

$$\frac{\text{Current Assets}}{\text{Current Liabilities}} = \frac{510,862}{163,679} = 3.12$$

The Current Ratio tells you how many dollars should be available in the next 12 months to pay the liabilities that will mature in the next 12 months. This example shows that $3.12 is available for each $1.00 in liabilities. A healthy current ratio.

A rule of thumb is $2 for each $1.00. Many small companies are struggling at a $1.00-to-$1.00 ratio or less.

QUICK RATIO:

$$\frac{\text{Cash \& Accounts Receivable}}{\text{Current Liabilities}} = \frac{182,559 + 146,281}{163,679} = 2.00$$

The Quick Ratio gives an indication of how quickly a company can pay its current obligations without relying on future sales. This example indicates a very healthy company, however, a $1-to-$1 ratio is a good basic ratio.

Most quick ratios I've seen in small companies are less, 75-cents-to-$1.00; or 75 cents available to pay $1.00 worth of liabilities without relying on future sales. As this ratio gets smaller, you will find that paying bills will become more and more difficult.

DEBT TO EQUITY:

$$\frac{\text{Total Debt}}{\text{Total Equity}} = \frac{193,073}{553,907} = .35$$

The Debt to Equity Ratio is the ratio that compares the amount invested in the business by creditors versus the amount invested by owners.

When securing bank financing, this is an important ratio. Many banks will have a policy that will prevent them from loaning your company money if this ratio goes beyond certain levels. In the example that was given, the .35-to-1 ratio is extremely low. This may indicate that the owner of the company is not taking advantage of the availability of borrowing for possible business expansion or realizing his full business potential.

Most small businesses will have a 3-to-1 or larger ratio. This results from the fact that most small businesses are under-funded by the owners and must continuously borrow.

As this ratio gets larger and larger it may be an indication that the company may have difficulty paying its debt and is in trouble.

NET INCOME TO EQUITY:

$$\frac{\text{Net Income}}{\text{Stockholders' Equity}} = \frac{119{,}487}{553{,}907} = .22$$

The Net Income to Equity Ratio indicates the return on the investment (ROI) that the shareholders are receiving based on the equity they have in the business. In the example given, the shareholders are receiving a 22 percent return on the equity remaining in the business.

A more appropriate measure of the return on investment would be to adjust the shareholders' equity from book value to market value by adjusting the assets of the business for any increase or decrease in their value. For example, in the company we are analyzing, if you look in the property and equipment section, you see they own land which is being carried at $126,150. If the land substantially appreciated to, let's say, a value of $500,000, then the book value of the company should be adjusted for this appreciation. This increases the book value by the differences between $126,150 and $500,000 or $373,850. This means that in calculating the return on investment, you should be taking $373,850 (the increase in the value of the land) plus the net equity, $553,907 totalling $927,757, divided into the earnings of $119,487, indicating a return on investment of 12.9 percent. Quite a difference from the rate of return calculated before adjusting for the appreciation in assets.

Recently I spoke with some people who had a business that was producing approximately $25,000 per year of annual income. Many years prior to this, they had purchased real property that was occupied by their business. The real property had increased substantially, and when asked the value, they indicated it was approximately $750,000. They were using $750,000 in real estate to produce $25,000 in income which meant that they were getting a return on the real estate of approximately 3 percent. To have a better utilization of their assets, they should have sold the real estate or developed it for another use and moved their company to quarters that were less expensive. Those businesses that are unincorporated and wish to determine the return on their investment must remember that the net income of their sole proprietorship or partnership should be reduced by reasonable compensation to the owners to determine the true net income to be used in the calculation.

INVENTORY TURNOVER:

$$\frac{\text{Cost of Goods Sold}}{\text{Inventory}} = \frac{778,082}{160,993} = 4.8 \text{ times}$$

The Inventory Ratio is the number of times that a business turns inventory during the year. In this example, the inventory turns 4.8 times.

To determine how many days of inventory you have on hand at any given time, divide the number computed into the number of days in the accounting period. For example, since the financial statement we are analyzing is for one year, we took 360 divided by 4.8 and it indicates approximately 75 days of inventory on hand.

When a company becomes more complex, and you choose to calculate profit and loss by inventory lines, this ratio can become a more valuable tool in determining understocking, overstocking, and obsolescence of inventory by product.

Many companies try to strive for the most turnovers within an operating cycle. Be cautious with this approach. To increase your inventory turnover you must reduce the amount of inventory on hand, and this might result in lower sales if you have an insufficient amount of goods available for sale to customers.

NET INCOME TO NET SALES:

$$\frac{\text{Net Income}}{\text{Net Sales}} = \frac{119{,}487}{1{,}336{,}454} = 8.9$$

The Net Income to Net Sales Ratio indicates how many dollars of profit you earn from each dollar of sales made. In the example, for every dollar of sales, the company earns 8.9 cents profit.

ACCOUNTS RECEIVABLE TURNOVER:

$$\frac{\text{Net Sales}}{\text{Accounts Receivable}} = \frac{1{,}336{,}454}{146{,}281} = 9.1$$

The Accounts Receivable Turnover indicates how many times the accounts receivable are being paid and re-established during the accounting period. The higher the turnover, the faster the collections.

To determine the number of days' sales that are in accounts receivable, take the ratio derived and divide it into the number of days in the accounting period. For example, since this is a year, we will use 360 days divided by 9.1 which indicates we have approximately 40 days' sales in accounts receivable. This is a healthy rate. Most small companies have anywhere from 60 to 70 or more days' sales in accounts receivable. What is yours?

The collection of accounts receivable is critical. Keep a close eye on this ratio. If it begins to indicate that collections are slowing down, take strong action to improve the company's collection policies.

ACCOUNTS PAYABLE TURNOVER:

$$\frac{\text{Purchases}}{\text{Accounts Payable}} = \frac{792{,}362}{94{,}272} = 8.4$$

The Accounts Payable Turnover indicates the number of times accounts payable will be paid during the year. To determine the number of days a business will take to pay its bills, divide the amount indicated, 8.4, into the number of days in the accounting period. As our example is one year, we will use 360 days, thus indicating that the accounts payable are being paid every 43 days.

If you look at the accounts receivable turnover, the example indicates 40 days. Compare this to the accounts payable turnover, which is every 43 days. You can see that the company is paying its bills more slowly than it is collecting its accounts receivable. In effect, the company is borrowing from its suppliers to expand its working capital.

These analyses are intended to help you understand financial statements. As your business becomes more sophisticated and your statements more complex, talk to your accountant. He will be best prepared to discuss their meaning.

Sample
Financial
Statement

(A) YOUR COMPANY, INC.
BALANCE SHEET

As of _____

ASSETS

(1) CURRENT ASSETS

Cash	$ 182,559	
Accounts receivable—trade, net		
of allowance for doubtful accounts	146,281	
Inventory	160,933	
Prepaid expenses	12,120	
Deferred taxes	8,969	
TOTAL CURRENT ASSETS		$ 510,862

(2) PROPERTY AND EQUIPMENT—At Cost

Automobiles	13,428	
Office furniture and equipment	10,867	
Plant machinery and equipment	125,019	
Leasehold improvements	8,579	
Land	126,150	
	284,043	
Less accumulated depreciation	109,045	174,998

(3) OTHER ASSETS

Investments	45,305	
Deposits	2,050	
Cash surrender value of officers'		
life insurance	13,765	61,120
TOTAL ASSETS		$ 746,980

LIABILITIES AND STOCKHOLDERS' EQUITY

(4) CURRENT LIABILITIES

Accounts payable	$ 94,272	
Accrued expenses	49,602	
Payroll and sales taxes payable	7,308	
Current portion of long-term debt	9,798	
Income taxes payable	2,699	
TOTAL CURRENT LIABILITIES		$ 163,679

(5) LONG-TERM DEBT, Net of Current Portion Above   29,394

TOTAL LIABILITIES   193,073

(6) STOCKHOLDERS' EQUITY

Common stock, no par value; 25,000 shares authorized, 3,180 shares issued and outstanding		$ 3,180	
Retained earnings:			
Balance—July 1, 19XX	$ 431,240		
Net income for the year ended June 30, 19XX	119,487	550,727	553,907
TOTAL LIABILITIES AND STOCKHOLDERS' EQUITY			$ 746,980

(B) YOUR COMPANY, INC.
STATEMENT OF INCOME
For the Period Ended _____

		Amount	%
(1) SALES		$ 1,336,454	100.0
(2) COST OF GOODS SOLD			
Beginning inventory	$ 146,653		
Purchases	792,362		
Total available	939,015		
Less ending inventory	160,933	778,082	58.2
(3) GROSS PROFIT		558,372	41.8
(4) SELLING AND ADMINISTRATIVE EXPENSES			
Selling expense	23,172		
Administrative expense	88,031	111,203	8.3
INCOME BEFORE OTHER INCOME		447,169	33.5
OTHER INCOME		6,484	.4
(5) INCOME BEFORE OFFICERS' COMPENSATION		453,653	33.9
(6) OFFICERS' COMPENSATION			
Salaries	250,600		
Officers' life insurance	1,566	252,166	18.9
(7) INCOME BEFORE PROVISION FOR INCOME TAXES		201,487	15.0
PROVISION FOR INCOME TAXES		82,000	6.1
(8) NET INCOME		$ 119,487	8.9

(C) YOUR COMPANY, INC.
STATEMENT OF CHANGES IN FINANCIAL POSITION
For the Period Ended _____

(1)	SOURCES OF CASH	
	Operations:	
(2)	Net income	$ 119,487
(3)	Add (subtract) items not requiring outlay of cash:	14,001
	Depreciation:	133,488
(4)	Other items affecting cash from operations:	
	Decrease in accounts receivable	1,179
	(Increase) in inventory	(14,280)
	(Increase) in prepaid expenses	(6,008)
	Increase in accounts payable	53,108
	(Decrease) in accrued expenses	(7,340)
	(Decrease) in payroll and sales tax payable	(3,368)
	Increase in income taxes payable	1,217
(5)	CASH PROVIDED BY OPERATIONS	157,996
	Decrease in:	
	Due from officers	1,120
(6)	TOTAL CASH PROVIDED	159,116
(7)	USES OF CASH	
	Purchase of plant machinery and equipment	37,978
	Repayment of debt	66,834
	Increase in:	
	Cash surrender value of officers' life insurance	1,851
(8)	TOTAL CASH USED	106,663
	INCREASE IN CASH DURING YEAR	52,453
(9)	CASH—Beginning of Year	130,106
	CASH—End of Year	$ 182,559

(D)   YOUR COMPANY, INC.
SCHEDULE OF SELLING AND ADMINISTRATIVE EXPENSES
For the Period Ended _____

	Amount	%
SELLING EXPENSES		
Advertising	$ 1,645	.1
Automobile	12,238	.9
Conventions	170	—
Commissions	4,532	.3
Freight-out	765	.1
Insurance	1,606	.1
Promotion	1,566	.1
Travel	650	.1
TOTAL SELLING EXPENSES	$ 23,172	1.7
ADMINISTRATIVE EXPENSES		
Bad debts	$ 4,303	.3
Dues and subscriptions	370	—
Employee benefits	1,102	.1
Interest	4,257	.2
Janitors	1,924	.2
Office	2,783	.2
Professional fees	10,681	.8
Profit-sharing plan	48,308	3.6
Relocation	881	.1
Repairs	167	—
Rent	2,612	.2
Salaries-office	5,035	.4
Taxes and licenses	527	—
Taxes—payroll	784	.1
Telephone	4,297	.3
TOTAL ADMINISTRATIVE EXPENSES	$ 88,031	6.5

9
We Must Plan for the Future

I RECEIVED A CALL from an old friend, Rob Jenkins, who indicated he needed my opinion on a business matter and wanted to see me. "Come on over," I said. About one half-hour later, we met in the lobby of my office.

Rob, a young man in his early 40s, wears a full beard, and was sporting a fresh tan. He is always impeccably dressed. Great taste, I thought to myself, right out of a Gucci ad. We proceeded to my office, sat down, and started with our usual small talk.

When the small talk ended, Rob opened a Pandora's box. "My lawyer says I should take my company public," he said. "Frankly, I'm concerned that he may be giving me this advice because of the substantial legal fees involved. I need your objective opinion."

"How can you take your company public when you just sold off 25 locations?"

"No problem," he retorted, "we're buying them back."

Ouch, I thought to myself, sell them, buy them back—what's he doing? "A year ago you indicated that you wanted to get smaller."

"Yeah, but now I want to make a killing. And besides, you know I've been unhappy with my partner for years, and this may give me the opportunity to get him out."

"Rob, you confuse me. Every six months you've changed your mind; expand and open more locations, franchise, don't franchise, sell locations, become smaller, sell out, merge, go public, make the big bucks, settle for a substantial living."

"Forget that," he said, "I know all about our previous discussions; what do you think?"

"Rob, your lawyer is giving you sound advice, but what is your opinion? It's your company."

Rob hemmed and hawed and concluded with his typical "no decision" decision. We ended our meeting and off Rob went, I presume to "go public." We've had countless discussions of this nature over the past five years. Rob's been hard to keep up with.

Larry Jacobs surprised me when he stuck his head in the door of my office. Larry just celebrated his 50th birthday and has been in the manufacturing business for 20 years. "Hi," I said, peering over the top of my glasses. "What's up?"

"I'm in deep trouble, and things are just terrible. A hope and a prayer is all I have between me and bankruptcy."

Good grief, I thought, 20 years in business and look where he's at.

One evening I was waiting for a table in a restaurant, when suddenly I felt a hand grab my shoulder. I whirled around and was facing Don Altman. "My God, I haven't seen you in months," I said. "How are you?"

"Fine, just fine. Let me introduce you to my wife." His wife and I smiled. We both knew we had been formally introduced on ten different occasions.

Don and his father had been in the retail business for years. 1981 and 1982 had been very tough business years for them. Sales were down and stores had been closed. It must have been a nightmare. I asked Don if his business problems had settled down. "You know we shrunk from ten to two stores, it's probably just a matter of time when we'll have to sell out. The administrative overhead is still killing us, and I can't get it any lower."

"Is Wally (Don's unproductive alter ego) still working with you?"

"Oh yeah, $40,000 a year to run one store."

"You're still paying him $40,000?"

"Yeah, how can I let him go? He's been with us for years."

"What good is loyalty if you are out of business?" I asked.

Lowering his head he replied, "I know, I know. By the way, do you think you could reduce your fee by about $50 a month? It sure will help."

I looked at him and said, "Here's $50 worth of advice. Get rid of Wally. Bankruptcy won't help anyone."

A few days later, I was sitting in my office, feet propped up on the desk, and I was wondering what the hell was going on. Here was Rob Jenkins off and running with his company in several directions depending on his mood swings. The company's sales were down and profits had shrunk considerably. Yet he still couldn't make up his mind about where he wanted his company to go. Larry Jacobs turned down establishing a financial plan to sustain what resources he had left and Don Altman watches his company get smaller and smaller with his $40,00-per-year sidekick.

Can't they see a "hope and a prayer" isn't the answer? They are lacking direction. They need a well thought out plan to guide their company's future. In good or bad times, the old "seat of the pants" planning doesn't work anymore.

Jenkins, Altman, and Jacobs may appear to be extreme examples yet they are the rule rather than the exception. Most small concerns have minimal, if any, concrete plans for the future. The planning process does not exist.

Most owner-managers of small companies have become so inundated with the day-to-day details and problem solving that when one mentions planning for the future, they throw up their hands and shout, "Who has time?"

My observation is that there *is* time, but planning for the future is such an abstract concept that people don't take the time to do it.

THE FIVE-YEAR PLAN: FORGET IT!

I recently had the opportunity to speak at UCLA as part of a business planning seminar. Fortunately, I was the last speaker at an all-day seminar. Can you imagine eight hours on how to prepare your business plan?

I arrived late, saving myself from the profound advice given by lawyers, underwriters, and other accountants. If it takes eight hours to learn how to prepare a business plan, we'll never do it.

The experts tell us that a five-year plan must be done. Yet, who can worry about five years in the future when cash is short, sales are down, and interest rates are killing us? The future is elusive. It never comes.

First, let's get rid of the notion of a five-year plan. Don't do one. It's too abstract, difficult, and too time-consuming. Let's do it the easy way so we can develop *some* kind of plan. What is needed is a written business plan that will allow us to measure our activities against established goals, and judge whether we are on the path to success or failure.

There are two kinds of plans needed in today's economic environment. The first, the subject of this chapter, is an operational plan to guide your company. The second, to be discussed in the next chapter, is a personal plan to protect your most important personal asset.

THE WINE AND CHEESE BUSINESS PLAN

To prepare your operational business plan—remember, this is going to establish your company's goals—we need five things: (1) a pencil, (2) a pad of legal size yellow paper, (3) a financial advisor, accountant, banker, lawyer, or anybody who has good business sense (we just eliminated the banker and the lawyer), (4) a package of cheese, and (5) a large bottle of wine: white, or red rosé, it makes no difference.

Once you have gathered the five items, it will be necessary to establish the proper setting. This can be your office, home, or any place that will be quiet and free from distractions. Your planning session should be scheduled after business hours when the phone has stopped ringing.

Follow these four simple steps, and you are on your way to experiencing your first wine-and-cheese planning session and establishing your company's goals and directions.

STEP 1—POUR A LITTLE WINE

Uncork the wine and pour a large glass, take a swig, and eat the cheese at will.

STEP 2—ASK QUESTIONS

Start to ask questions at random regarding various aspects of your business. This is a thinking-out-loud session with your financial advisor. As you ask the questions, write them down. Everything must be written down because verbalizing alone is useless. You will never remember what you've discussed. By the way, don't forget to offer the advisor some wine and cheese.

One typical question you might start with is: What kind of business am I in? Sounds like a silly question, but one that should not be overlooked.

Boyd Reiter started his business by importing stereo equipment from Japan. Then he started to export stereo equipment to South America. When the bicycle craze hit he imported bicycles, then jeans. He started manufacturing fishing equipment in Korea and electronic levels in Hong Kong. When he was last seen, he was in New Jersey hiding from creditors. Hey, Boyd, what business were you in?

During this session, a major area to consider is your cash needs. How much cash will you need in the future? When will you run out of cash? Where will you get the cash? Bankers? Partner? Public? Profits? Or use your own? These questions lead to the need for doing cash forecasting, a projection of your future cash needs. This is a must for any business plan. However, don't do your cash forecasting in this session. It requires a lot of details and should be prepared, with your input, by your bookkeeper, accountant, or anybody you trust with the information (see Chapter 7).

After you've had a couple of glasses of wine you'll probably find the questions come a lot easier.

STEP 3—WRITE DOWN YOUR ANSWERS

As you and your advisor toss questions and answers back and forth, jot them down. Don't worry about grammar and refinement of your answers, just write them down.

THE QUESTIONS

One word of caution. After you've read the questions provided, you may be tempted to just write answers to these questions. Don't. The free-wheeling dialogue that can develop between you and your advisor will produce greater results.

There are numerous areas to cover during your wine-and-cheese planning session. You may choose to break them down into the following categories: production, marketing, personnel, facilities, and money.

WHAT BUSINESS AM I IN?

As I indicated earlier, this may seem ridiculous at first. However, it is not unusual to see some businesses going in several directions and not precisely defining what business activity they choose to emphasize.

PRODUCING THE PRODUCT

1. Do I know precisely what my product costs?
2. Will I need a cost accounting system?
3. What are the advantages of producing my own product?
4. What are the disadvantages?
5. What are the advantages of having others produce my product?
6. What are the disadvantages of having others produce my product?

7. Should I manufacture my product or go outside and have others manufacture my product?
8. Should I manufacture it domestically or abroad?
9. What processes do I eventually want automated?
10. Is my plant layout adequate?
11. If my plant layout is not adequate, how will I improve it?
12. Is my equipment obsolete?
13. If my equipment is obsolete, what new equipment do I expect to buy in the future?
14. Is the labor force in this area fulfilling my needs?
15. Are labor costs reasonable?
16. In what direction do I anticipate my future material costs going?
17. Is there an abundant supply of material available?
18. How can I control future costs?
19. Am I buying properly?
20. What can I do to take advantage of discounts?
21. How can I increase my gross margin?
22. Is the demand for my product strong?
23. How can I improve the production of my product or service in the future?

The questions listed above are only the beginning. The dialogue between you and your advisor is needed to expand the scope of your inquiry. If the process is getting overwhelming, stop. Go out for a walk to relax. If your head is beginning to feel scrambled, that's a good sign. It indicates that you are doing some real, creative thinking.

MARKETING

1. Where will I get future business from?
2. Will I stay local, regional, or become national?
3. Will I advertise?
4. Should I use an ad agency?
5. Should I hire a public relations firm?
6. Should I do media advertising—television, newspaper, radio?
7. How much money should I spend on marketing in the future?
8. Will I need a sales manager?
9. Are my distributors adequate?

10. Should I change distributors or hire additional distributors?
11. Will I need brochures, advertising products, samples?
12. When is the best time for me to do my advertising?
13. What results do I expect from my advertising?
14. Is my showroom adequate?
15. Are my displays adequate?
16. Are my window trimmings adequate?
17. Am I using proper methods for submitting bids?
18. Who is the best person in my organization to be meeting with prospective customers?
19. Are my sales personnel trained adequately in the process of selling?
20. Are there trade associations I should join?

PERSONNEL

1. Are my personnel adequate for my future needs?
2. Am I training personnel properly?
3. Am I giving personnel adequate responsibility?
4. What training programs or training facilities will I utilize in the future to assist in the training of personnel?
5. Will I need to expand the number of personnel in various departments throughout the organization?
6. What criteria will I use for determining who, when, and how to hire or fire?
7. Do I have adequate personnel manuals?
8. Do I have appropriate fringe benefits?
9. Are my salaries competitive?
10 Do I have proper recruiting techniques?
11. Am I following all the laws with regard to personnel?
12. Will I need a personnel director?
13. Will I need a greater level of expertise within our personnel?
14. How will I acquire this?
15. Are my personnel growing as the company is growing?
16. Am I capable of motivating personnel?
17. Do I display appropriate respect for personnel in my dealings with them?

18. Is there an adequate review procedure to keep personnel informed of their progress within the organization?
19. Are the top levels of management able to function when I'm not around?
20. Do I encourage my employees to be creative and innovative?
21. As the leader of the company, am I accessible?

FACILITIES AND ADMINISTRATION

1. Are my facilities adequate for my future needs?
2. If they are not, will I buy or lease?
3. Where will I relocate?
4. When should I be planning for any future changes in location of facilities?
5. Will I need a purchasing agent?
6. Will I need a cost accountant?
7. Will I need a controller?
8. Is my accounting firm adequate?
9. Are my lawyers capable?
10. Is my rent reasonable?
11. How can I reduce my communication costs?
12. How can I reduce my administrative costs?
13. Do I need an office manager?
14. Are my plant and facilities well organized?
15. Am I using appropriate modern equipment?
16. Am I well insured?
17. Should I incorporate or unincorporate?

MONEY

1. How much money will I need in the future? This question leads to the need for doing a cash budget and/or forecast. These are a must in any business plan. Refer to Chapter 7. No plan is complete without the answer to this question. Do not attempt to answer this question in your first session. It will require some detailed pencil pushing.
2. When will I run out of money? All small and medium-sized businesses will run short of cash during different times in the

business cycle. Preparation in advance for this inevitability is a must.

3. Where will I get money to cover my future needs?
   A. Bankers?
   B. Partner?
   C. Investor?
   D. Go public?
   E. My own money?
   F. Other financial institutions?
4. What will I need to prepare for a financial presentation to a prospective financier? The answer to this question is simple. You will need the following:
   A. A business plan (see page 125 for the contents of a business plan).
   B. Reviewed or audited financial statements of the company.
   C. Personal financial statements.
   D. A projection covering future earnings and proposed activity.

ONLY THE BEGINNING

All of these questions are only the beginning. This kind of planning and thinking out loud is a must to get your company moving forward.

STEP 4—THE NEXT DAY

When you have completed the session, two things will have occurred. One, you are probably feeling no pain, and two, you've actually worked out a business plan. This plan will provide goals and direction for you and your company.

After you have taken two aspirin, start thinking about what you've prepared. Do the questions and answers make sense? If you conclude that you've set the right direction and the process is meaningful, bring in others from within your company to seek their input and ideas. Not only should you get some valuable ideas from them, but this could be the start of a new method of dialogue between you and your staff leading to a stronger management team.

Begin to rewrite or restate the questions you've discussed.

Define the answers with the input of others and lay out the plan in logical sequence. Develop a tentative time frame for the implementation of each phase.

Once you have satisfied yourself that your plan is completed, give a copy to all the personnel in your organization who will be responsible for its implementation. This will give them a better understanding of where your company is going and a greater sense of participation in the company's future.

THE BUSINESS PLAN FOR RAISING CAPITAL

The wine-and-cheese operational business plan is to be used for setting goals and directions for your company. These goals can be used by management for measuring short-term results and for providing short-term guidance for the decision-making process.

Often companies need to develop a broader business plan that gives long range goals and ideas to convey the overall philosophy and direction of the company. These plans are used to secure capital through loans, private financing and/or venture capital.

A WELL-PREPARED BUSINESS PLAN . . .

- helps management delineate objectives, directions, and strategies.
- helps company officials reach a consensus about the company's future.
- gains the confidence of existing and potential investors.
- shows major suppliers your ability to pay.
- persuades potential customers to place orders by showing your ability to deliver.
- convinces bankers, investors, and other capital sources that your company has planned for its financial success.

A SUCCESSFUL BUSINESS PLAN . . .

- is prepared or reviewed by outside parties (such as a CPA, management consultant, or attorney).
- shows projected financing and how it will work for the company.

- contains a well-written narrative and set of financial projections showing the company's projected financial condition, net income, and cash flow.
- is prefaced by a concise summary which serves as an appetizer for the reader to continue reading.
- provides a tool for later comparison with actual operating results.
- contains all essential disclosures necessary for the reader's decision about your company.
- must be adapted for the specific company.
- is recognized as a dynamic planning tool, subject to change.
- is well written for the potential investor or creditor who is not familiar with the company's past or future operations.

OUTLINE OF A BUSINESS PLAN

The following outline of a typical business plan is intended only to serve as a skeleton guide. There is no such thing as a typical company; therefore any standard outline must be adapted to your specific needs. When preparing a business plan, carefully identify and describe the characteristics which make your company different. Highlight those characteristics, and be realistic.

The heart of the business plan is a set of financial projections showing the bank or investor how effective you will be with their money.

THE COMPANY

- This section whets the reader's appetite and should be short and concise.
- Incorporation and location (indicate number of employees, etc.)
- Describe products and current stage of development.
- Summarize activities to date.
- Briefly outline the unrealized potential of the company. Be honest. Be realistic.
- Required financing. Be realistic.
- Use of the financing proceeds. Show where the money will go.

- Return on investment.
- Licensing or other agreements of value.

SELECTED FINANCIAL INFORMATION

- Your outside accountants can be helpful in the preparation of this section.
- Include a synopsis of the company's operating results to date.
- This section should include a summary of the results of projections of the future operations of the company if the financing plan being proposed is successful.

FACTORS TO CONSIDER

- Include a short, concise statement listing risks to be considered.
- If the company is just starting operations, then a brief narration of its limited operations should be discussed.
- Transactions entered into by the company and related parties should be disclosed, i.e., sales with shareholders, loans to shareholders, etc.
- Operational losses to date (if appropriate).
- Conflicts of interest.
- Applicable government regulations.
- Restrictions on stock transfers or the ability to trade equity securities.
- Loan covenants.
- Dependence on key individuals.
- Requirements for additional financing.
- Dilution of interest because original promoters invested at lower per share amounts.
- Other uncertainties and risks.
  Note: While you may believe that citations of risks may negatively affect an investor's or banker's opinion of the company, it conveys an appearance of honesty and lends credibility to the business plan. Furthermore, if appropriate, the remainder of the business plan should mitigate the identified risks.
- Competition in the field.

USE OF PROCEEDS

If the business plan is to be used to acquire capital (e.g., sales of stock or bank loans), show a schedule of major areas of proceeds uses, followed by a brief textual discussion of each major use. For example, list uses for:

- Marketing
- Research and Development
- Working capital (breakdown by accounts receivable, inventory, etc.)
- Advertising and promotion
- Equipment and facilities
- Retirement of debt
- Expansion of operations
- Other important uses

PRODUCTS OR SERVICES

- Describe in detail products manufactured or sold to date by the company.
- Show the historical expansion of product lines and other key operational activities.
- Summarize your intended expansion of product lines.
- List any license agreement related to products.
  Note: Emphasize how your products differ from those of your competitors. Highlight quality, advanced engineering, product appeal to customers, and customer satisfaction.

MARKETING

- Describe your marketing plans. Your marketing consultants may be able to assist in the writing of this section.
- Outline your company's economic base, who you serve and want to serve (by age, sex, industry, etc.).
- Describe the image of your products and service in the eyes of users.
- Summarize marketing and promotion strategy to date.

- Show how marketing has been performed to date (in-house, dealers, distributors, etc.).
- Discuss briefly the market trends and other market data used in marketing decisions.
- Note any intended changes in marketing and promotion strategy.
- Show anticipated benefits of changes in marketing and promotion strategy.
- Name competitors (on a national, regional or local basis) and the advantages or disadvantages you enjoy, and will enjoy, after carrying out marketing plans.
- Show reaction of customers.

MANAGEMENT

- List the officers and directors of the company.
- Describe their backgrounds, highlighting their experience in related fields.

FINANCIAL STATEMENTS

- Historical operations

PROJECTIONS—A LOOK AT THE COMPANY'S FUTURE

Note: Although projections may be the last item in the package, they are the heart of the plan. They should be highlighted and referred to frequently in the text of the business plan. (see the sample business plan in the appendix).

10
Personal Planning Is a Must

MOST OF US consider personal planning tantamount to a proper estate plan, good tax planning, setting up pension and profit sharing plans, making wise investments, and being adequately insured. In other words, doing everything necessary to keep our hands on what we earn and build an estate for future needs.

This kind of planning is complex and should be done with the help of a good professional advisor. Do not do your estate and tax planning alone. Hire a pro.

YOUR MOST VALUABLE ASSET

It was January 31, 1964, and I was experiencing my first tax season as an accountant. I was standing in a large brightly lit room containing rows of desks where people sat, heads bowed, working over stacks of papers. This is what is commonly referred to in the accounting profession as a "bull pen," a very sterile, functional work area packed with people. The back of my neck was killing me and I ached all over. It was 7:30 p.m. and I couldn't wait to leave. The aching was unbearable.

I left at 8:30 p.m., got home, and my wife asked me if I'd like some dinner. "No, hon, I just want to lie down and rest." And rest I did. Three days later I awoke and was rushed to the isolation ward of a nearby hospital. I had mononucleosis *and* hepatitis. It would be two and one-half months before I would return to work. April 16, to be exact—great planning? There went my first tax season.

If you know anything about mono, as it's called, it's a condition that makes one sleep. The body is so exhausted that sleep is all you want to do and are able to do.

Yet, I was so worried and distraught about my loss of income, that after my initial three days of sleep and exhaustion, I started to have sleepless nights worrying about where the money would come from to support my wife and family. My wife was working, but when my checks stopped coming in, it cut our income in half. Because of those sleepless nights, the doctors started to give me sleeping pills to rest. Here I was suffering from a disease that makes one sleep, and yet I was taking sleeping pills to sleep. The power of a worried mind is incredible.

WHAT WILL HAPPEN TO YOUR BUSINESS?

How much thought have you given to the status of your business if you're not there for a sustained period of time? How many sleepless nights will you have? Take a look around you. Will your company personnel keep it going? Will you continue to receive your income? Will the business continue or is it finished because of your absence? Who will collect the accounts receivable? Who will keep the equipment running? Who will take customer orders? Buy goods? Maintain inventory? Watch cash flow? Pay bills?

GOOD PEOPLE WILL MAKE THE DIFFERENCE

The most important and valuable asset in your company is highly trained and responsible employees. Your survival will depend on trained people. All the devices of high technology are worthless unless you have good people. An investment in people is as important as an investment in equipment. Good people help us survive. Yet, time and time again, I have heard owners of small companies say that "employees are a pain in the ass, they drive me crazy." If you complain about your employees in this manner, take a hard look at who hired them. The buck stops with you. Good people will make the difference.

WE MUST DELEGATE AND TRAIN

The primary purpose of delegating is to allow owner-managers suffi-cient time to manage their company. Your time needs to be spent controlling company expenses, monitoring the key financial elements of the company, learning to understand what the company's financial statements mean, and planning for the future. Delegation is also the key element in the development and training of responsible employees.

WHY DO WE RESIST DELEGATING?

The owner-managers of small companies tend not to delegate for several reasons.

Incompetent staff. When we fail to have confidence in subordinates, we will not delegate to them. This can be overcome by hiring better people, providing training, and making certain that those people who are incompetent are let go.

The glory of manual labor. A major portion of the functions of the owner-manager are mental rather than physical. Often using one's brain is not considered working, thus we tend to do physical or manual labor rather than spending time thinking. We attract as much paperwork as we can to keep working.

The goal of the owner-manager should be to work their way out of work. There is no glory in doing it all.

I can do it better myself. This notion is so ingrained in the personality of the individual who follows it that it is extremely difficult to change. You may or may not be able to do it better yourself, but there is only so much you can do. Your company will never grow beyond your capabilities. If you are guilty of this, let go of it. It's limiting your growth and your company's.

Just starting out. Often when an individual is just starting in business they find that their role is that of "chief cook and bottle washer." They do everything. There is a lack of sufficient resources to hire people and delegate.

When starting in business this is generally the case and not much can be done about it. However, an integral part of what you do, even though you're just starting out, must include the strategies outlined throughout this book.

MAKE A LIST

Get a small pocket note pad and carry it with you at all times. Every day for the next two weeks, jot down on this note pad all activities in which you have participated. Try to do this contemporaneously with the activity and be as detailed and specific as possible.

After two weeks, have the items on your list typed and numbered. Review the list and place a check mark alongside each activity that could have been performed by some other individual in your organization.

Count the number of checks and compare them to the number of entries. By dividing the number of checks by the number of entries, you will have the percentage of work you do that could have been performed by others. If you have 140 entries and 75 check marks, 54 percent of your work could have been performed by somebody else (140 divided by 75 = 54 percent).

MAKE ASSIGNMENTS

After you have reviewed your list and decided which tasks to delegate, decide who in your company is best suited for carrying them out. The assignment should be in writing and you must inform all relevant personnel whom you have chosen to perform the task.

After the assignment has been made and you have informed the appropriate personnel, begin the training.

TRAINING BEGINS AT THE TOP

As an accountant, I have reviewed the financial statements of many,

many companies. Consistently I have found few dollars, if any, spent on education. Why do we follow the notion that once we are in business, the process of formal education stops and the school of hard knocks takes over?

Our society and businesses have become so complex that the process of education must continue. The greatest idea, product, or process goes nowhere without highly educated and responsible people.

Remember Ernie Houseman, whose business was expanding? He was so inundated with detail that he was functioning as a clerk. Ernie was a trained chemist with no business education. One night a week Ernie attended class at UCLA studying anthropology. He enjoyed the break from his business routine but why wasn't he attending a class in managerial skills?

Continuing education must begin at the top. The highest levels of management must be continuously educated and re-educated to keep up with the ever-changing concepts and theories of management in today's changing environment.

We'll spend 12 to 14 hours a day running our business yet we'll spend so little time in learning the skills necessary for success. We spend little on our own formal training, and virtually nothing for the levels below. Here are some suggestions for successful training:

- Prepare the learner. Let them know this new knowledge will be of value to themselves and the company.
- Present the task. Make certain your explanations are clear and concise.
- Practice the job. Allow the employee to learn by setting aside time to practice. Their other work may be delayed while they are learning their new assignment. Be patient.
- Make certain the trainee is taking adequate notes.
- Have the right attitude. Create an atmosphere where fear and intimidation are not present. Allow people to make mistakes.
- Provide additional training. Use formal educational courses at all levels of your company. Attend trade association meetings and learn from your competitors.

- Always remember, new ideas generate new profits.
- Be patient.

PROTECT YOUR MOST VALUABLE ASSET

Highly educated and responsible employees are your most important asset. They will protect your business in the event of disability because your business will continue without interruption.

If one day you choose to retire, who better to purchase your interest than key employees? The key employees who have been trained and who are capable of continuing the company will allow you to reap the benefits of your company's value upon retirement.

One day you will die. Your heirs will be panicked. More than likely they will have very little knowledge of your business activity and pandemonium may be the order of the day. The business you have spent giving of your blood, sweat, and tears may have been of great value while you were alive, but what value on your death? Will an orderly liquidation or sale take place or will the business be over now that you're gone? Your educated and trained employees will make the difference between value and no value at all. The continuing education of you and your employees will be your strongest personal asset.

11
122 Minutes a Month Is All It Takes

ONCE THE SYSTEMS described in this book are in place, all it will take is 122 minutes of your time each month to monitor the results of your company's activity and give you a better understanding of your successes and/or failures. You will build a better business and make more money.

The Budget and Profit and Loss Statements . . . . 20 minutes
To review budget variances from the actual expenses on a line-by-line basis, and ask questions of those individuals in your organization who will have answers as to why the variances are there should take no more than 20 minutes each month. Of course, as the company gets larger and the financial statements and budgets grow more complex, this time may expand.

The Accounts Receivable . . . . 30 minutes
To review the aged accounts receivable and give collection instructions should take about 30 minutes each month. Before you get the listing of the accounts receivable, have your bookkeeper "red line" those customers that failed to pay during the month. This is the time to see who gets those nasty computer letters and a phone call from Bridget.

The Financial Statements . . . . 20 minutes
Have your bookkeeper prepare the ratio analysis from the descriptions in this book. Compare these ratios with the previous months to see if your financial position is improving.

Cash . . . . 52 minutes
Four minutes a day, 3 days a week, is all that is needed to check cash balances and review your two-week cash forecast. Keep your money working for you and have your bookkeeper or secretary prepare the two-week forecast.

Now that you have reduced your time in reviewing your company's financial activity to 122 minutes a month, you will have the time to spend an additional minute or two thinking about whether you are becoming a better manager.

As a better manager, you will control the expenses of the business by developing a budget and monitoring it monthly.

As a better manager, you will develop a management system to monitor financial statements, cash balances, accounts receivable, and inventories.

As a better manager, you will take the time necessary to do both personal and operational planning. These plans will give the company direction and develop a team to carry out company goals.

As a better manager, you will get involved in the community to acquire power and influence so as to become a community leader and have input in the political process that can make or break your company.

As a better manager, you will know that your attitude and style will be the spirit of the company, and that the company is a reflection of the people at the top, and **those people must be the best.**

12
How to Develop Power and Influence

NOW IS THE TIME for us to take stock of who we are and what we want. It's time to rid ourselves of the blanket of apathy and become involved. It is vitally important for you to realize that one of the specific functions you have as an owner-manager of your business is to develop as much power and influence as you can within your community.

This will enable you to get things done and have your voice heard when it counts. Your leadership must extend beyond the small confines of your company into the community at large. Your interests must be protected, and only you can protect them.

WHAT IS POWER AND INFLUENCE?

Power and influence means you have access to the leaders in your community and they have access to you. Power and influence is the ability to have dialogue with community leaders at all levels so you can have some input into the decisions they will make.

Our community leaders need your input. Unfortunately, most members of the small business community are so uninvolved that legislators consistently make laws without adequate information from this vital segment of our economy.

HOW DO YOU GET POWER AND INFLUENCE?

- Contribute to candidates and elected officials by attending dinner parties, cocktail parties, and other fundraising events. Make sure you have a few words with the candidate and the staff to let them know who you are.
- Meet staff members and field representatives of the officials and treat them well. Many times they may be calling the shots and will be of great assistance to you. It's not always necessary to have your problems solved directly by the politician. The staffs are a great help.
- Assist in raising funds. This is the most effective method. If you are one who has broken a few arms, held a few parties, and raised some bucks, this virtually guarantees access and the opportunity to have your opinions heard when it counts.
- Volunteer services. This helps but not to the same degree as raising money. My general observation is that those with the most dollars get the most.
- Keep your limited funds close to home. Don't try to go after presidential or senatorial influence. Your limited resources will be best used at the local levels. Most of the problems you will encounter will be local.
- Try to serve on committees that study issues affecting you and your industry. Remember, you are trying to give your opinion on issues that will affect you. Serving on committees is an excellent method to do so.
- Let people know of your involvement. You are going to need all the assistance you can get. This includes friends, relatives, and business associates. If you want to help the candidate of your choice, you're going to need your friends. Raising money is not easy, and you will have to get others to help you. Also, you should remember that help is a two-way street. Those people who have assisted you will call sooner or later. They will call sooner rather than later.
- Be informed. Don't always approach an issue purely from an emotional point of view. Know all aspects of an issue. Ranting and raving your concern is not as effective as an intelligent conversation.

HOW TO USE IT

If you've decided to become involved and make your voice heard, use your power and influence sparingly.

If you have a particular problem and you need help, try all avenues before approaching an elected official. Ultimately if you go to an elected official, make certain the problem is important. A favor used is gone forever.

Be realistic. Just because you've helped a legislator, don't expect miracles. You are one of many constituents.

Be very persistent if you believe in what you are doing.

Be wary of friends who seek your assistance in solving their problems. Is their problem important enough to you to use your access?

If you want something such as a committee assignment, an appointment, or a job, you've got to ask. Always assume that those who make assignments will not be clamoring at your door. You've got to tell them where the door is.

Our legislators need and welcome your input. All too often they become isolated from the realities of the world. They cannot legislate your needs and interests without you.

THE DIRECT APPROACH

A number of years ago I decided that I'd like some input into my own destiny. During my professional career I have seen the contempt, anger, and frustration that most people have in their dealings with government. I have concluded that much of this anger and frustration is self-inflicted and results from a rather complacent attitude—an attitude that manifests itself in a lack of involvement and concern and a notion that "you can't fight City Hall."

I wanted to get involved. I wanted my voice to be heard. No matter how insignificant that voice may be in the scheme of things, I wanted to have a voice in my own destiny. The burning question was how?

I decided to be direct. Across the hall from my office in Los Angeles was a public relations firm that was very active in political public relations. The firm's major client was Ronald Reagan. Michael Deaver, a principal in the firm, was one of Reagan's top aides.

I wrote Mike Deaver a note telling him that I was a Democrat who was interested in the Republican Party. It took Mike three months to respond. We ultimately arranged to have lunch.

During our lunch, I told him about myself and some Democratic friends who would like to become active in the Republican Party. To my delight, he suggested I arrange a luncheon in my office and invite some of those friends. He would invite Ronald Reagan to talk to us about the party and party politics.

Three weeks later we were sitting in my conference room, nine Democrats eating cold cuts from paper plates with the ex-Governor of California and the future President of the United States. We were in awe.

The meeting was a failure as far as getting involved in the party. Mike Deaver and Ronald Reagan were far too busy to help nine struggling Democrats become Republicans.

I had been dealing with small businesses for many years, and I had some ideas that I felt must be heard. So I decided to move onto the cocktail party circuit to "press the flesh" as they say.

While attending a cocktail party in honor of Ronald Reagan in 1979, I ran into a member of the Los Angeles School Board who was running for Congress. While talking to Representative Bobbi Fiedler (Republican-CA) about her plans, I mentioned I would be more than happy to attempt to raise a few dollars for her campaign. I was sure I had bitten off more than I could chew, because I had never raised money for a candidate at any time in my life. But I thought I'd give it a shot.

I managed to twist some arms, make some promises, and raise a few thousand dollars for the campaign. Fiedler eventually won the race by a slim margin and now I had a friend in Congress.

YOU TOO SHOULD HAVE A FRIEND OR FRIENDS IN CONGRESS

Think about it. There are literally thousands of bills before Congress each and every year. It requires almost superhuman skills on the part of our legislators to be informed about the bills they are asked to vote on.

Therefore, they rely on staffs, lobbyists, legislative leaders, and a multitude of others to supply the information they need to make reasonably intelligent decisions.

The people who have the access have the ability to filter information, have large organizations, and the time and money to be on the scene protecting their interests. This is usually big business, big unions, and highly influential special interest groups.

We, the owners and managers of small businesses, don't have the time, money or inclination to "fight City Hall." We can't afford to hire lobbyists and others to represent our interests. We are far too busy making our livings.

There are several effective small-business lobbying groups representing our interests, but far more often than not, they have a difficult time securing our support.

We are uninvolved and uninformed. Therefore, laws are made by members of legislative bodies who are informed by individuals with a point of view that often does not represent our interests.

CITIZEN LOBBYIST

I was standing in front of the Dirksen Senate Office Building in Washington D.C., trying to find a place to hide my half-smoked cigar.

Why do I do this, I thought. I always manage to light my cigar and take three puffs just prior to reaching my destination. If I take the smelly thing into the building they'll probably have to evacuate. So here I was standing in twenty degree weather looking for a safe hiding place for my cigar.

I spotted a small ledge near the entrance of the building and gently laid down my stogie making certain it would not roll off the ledge.

I proceeded through the heavy glass doors of the building and opened my briefcase so a guard could peek in to see what weapons I might be concealing. I had a meeting scheduled on the third floor with a legislative aide to a senator from the east coast. I was there to give my usual schpiel on the legislation I felt was needed to help the small business community. This had been one of many meetings in Washington over the last two years regarding this legislation.

The receptionist in the office informed me that Kathy Bayless would be returning from lunch any minute and offered me a magazine to pass the time.

Ten minutes later, Kathy appeared. She greeted me with a bright smile. She was a very attractive woman. I grabbed her hand and shook it briskly. She then guided me to a small cubicle and we proceeded to discuss the small business legislation.

"Did you receive the information my office sent?" I asked.

"Oh yes," she replied.

"Did you have the opportunity to read any of it?"

"No," she said.

They never do, I thought. I spent the next ten minutes extolling the virtues of the bill and why it was needed for the small business community. I completed my monologue and it was her turn.

"Why should we provide this kind of legislation for the small-business person?" she snapped. Before I could respond she continued, "They are the biggest tax cheaters in America."

I stared at her as anger began to swell within me. This had to be the most obnoxious comment I had heard. Fortunately, Kathy's attitude was the exception not the rule. Most of the people I had met had been fair, reasonable, and concerned with the fate of small business. But her attitude really got to me.

Kathy and I had a few more minutes of discussion while I managed to hold back my anger at her damn attitude. I left her office and headed for my next appointment in the building next door. I stepped into the cold afternoon air looking for the ledge where I had placed my cigar. I chuckled to myself. One frustration after the other, I thought. There was my cigar lying in a puddle of water, soaked clear through.

I started to walk toward the next building and began to think about why I was here. Three-thousand miles from home, cold and frustrated. It was amazing, I thought, a dramatic change had occurred in my life as a result of one rather insignificant event.

It was in 1979, when I had written an article for the *Los Angeles Business Journal*, "CPA Says Present Tax Laws Undermine Small Business." In the article I discussed the major problem small companies have—raising capital. I had suggested a tax incentive for a direct investment in a productive small business.

Presently, our tax laws allow valuable capital to chase unproductive tax shelters that create little real value for society. I felt that tax legislation must be adopted to provide capital to small productive businesses, where it belongs. However, I sat on the idea for two years after the article first appeared.

Mike Deaver once gave some advice about politics. He said, "Persistence pays off, so be persistent." Through my persistent efforts, Mike recommended my membership on the President's National Productivity Advisory Committee and, in 1981, President Reagan appointed me to this Committee. Our first meeting was held in January of 1982.

While in Washington, I decided to get some sense of what people thought of my idea for capital for small business. I presented the idea to representative Fiedler and staff members of other representatives. At the time, budgets and deficits were paramount on everybody's mind. They appeared to like the idea for a tax incentive for investment in a small business but "now is not the time."

Being persistent again as advised, I encouraged and finally persuaded Representative Fiedler and Representative Dan Marriott (R-Utah) to introduce the bill in June of 1982. The bill is called The Small Business Investment Incentive Act. It allows a small business to raise up to $250,000 by giving the investor a tax incentive for their direct investment in a small business.

After the bill had been introduced, passage became the goal and my many meetings in Washington began.

THE BILL—HELP, WE NEED HELP

The Small Business Investment Incentive Act allows a qualified small business to raise up to $250,000 for operations and expansion through the sale of its stock while permitting individual investors a deduction of up to $15,000 ($30,000 on a joint return) for the stock purchased in a small business. It has been estimated that over 100,000 new jobs will be created and that over one billion dollars will find its way into small business if this bill passes.

The Small Business Investment Incentive Act is presently in the House Ways and Means Committee in Congress awaiting their action. Please write to the members of the Ways and Means Committee and your Representatives in Congress urging them to support this needed legislation. Letters help so **write, write, write!**.

I have just been informed that the bill will be included in the Entrepreneurial Assistance and Tax Reform Act of 1985.

WHO BEST?

Who best to represent your interest than you? **Get involved.**

Appendix
A Sample
Business Plan

LOOSE GLOVES LTD.

IMPORT MANUFACTURER
FOR
LOOSE GLOVES

Prepared by the
Management Team
of
Loose Gloves Ltd.

2121 East Fifth Avenue, Cambridge, Massachusetts
(821) 342-6015   (777) 832-1021

TABLE OF CONTENTS
BUSINESS PLAN FOR LOOSE GLOVES

I. CORPORATE AND INDUSTRY OVERVIEW

II. COMPANY FORMATION
   A. Incorporation and Location
   B. Principal Product
   C. Activities to Date
   D. Unrealized Potential of Loose Gloves
   E. Required Financing
   F. Use of Funds
   G. Return on Investment

III. THE MARKETING PLAN
   A. Marketing Strategies—"Loosen up for Less"
   B. Pricing Strategy
   C. Sales Force
   D. Target Accounts
   E. Advertising and Promotions
   F. Brand Name Recognition
   G. Major Competitors' Strengths and Weaknesses

IV. SELECTED FINANCIAL INFORMATION
   A. Next 12 months Statement of Income
   B. Projected Balance Sheet after one year of operation.
   C. Projected Statement of Changes of Cash after one year of operations.

V. MANAGEMENT TEAM
   A. Organizational Chart
   B. Brief Biographies of Key Employees

VI. FACTORS TO CONSIDER

VII. PROJECTIONS—A LOOK AT THE COMPANY'S FUTURE

SECTION I   CORPORATE AND INDUSTRY OVERVIEW

A. The glove industry is a $2 billion growth-oriented marketplace that has experienced revolutionary growth and expansion over the last ten (10) years. The tremendous interest of the American consumer in fitness for both sexes has helped to perpetuate this growth.

In most growth-orientated industries, production innovation, heavy capital investment, and extensive R&D play a major growth role. However, the explosion in glove sales has occurred under these very unique circumstances:

1. The major United States companies have been marketing in the United States for less than fifteen (15) years.

2. In the past, the consumer wore the gloves known as "Tight Gloves" for all their glove needs. Today, we have a specialized market. Gloves are worn for running, tennis, racquetball, evening wear, snow skiing, gymnastics, driving, and cheer-leading.

3. Today's brand leaders are: 5 Fingers, Verytight Inc., Soft-gloves, Hold Hands, etc.

   a. 5 Fingers—started fourteen (14) years ago. Their current sales are $600 million plus their apparel division.

   b. Very Tight—$280 million, started in 1977.

   c. Soft Gloves—$100 million plus in seven (7) years.

   d. Hold Hands is the only leading manufacturer that is older and yet has seen its market share slip dramatically because of better marketing and merchandising by its new competition. Their sales today are $190 million.

4. Did you know that most of the above list, including 5 Fingers, do not manufacture any of their merchandise? It is all done by *Contract Manufacturing Firms* that build to order for the glove industry. These contract factories are in Taiwan, Korea, and certain countries in Europe.

5. Therefore, all but one (1) of the leading companies are Import/ Marketing firms who earned their share of the market by the quality of their marketing, designing, salesmanship, national advertising, and financial strength. Their manufacturing is done overseas.

6. **Loose Gloves Ltd.** holds the exclusive trademark and importing right to "Very Loose." We are the only glove company that can use the name "loose" on their glove.

7. The Loose line was designed and internationally marketed by Bill W. Smith (see biography in Sec. V), a ten-year design veteran of the glove industry, whose companies have offices in Switzerland and Taiwan. Mr. Smith and his supervisors coordinate all of the contract manufacturing of **Loose Gloves Ltd.** at five (5) different factories in Korea, Taiwan, and Italy for the international distribution of products to the world.

SECTION II   COMPANY FORMATION

A. **Loose Gloves Ltd.,** 2121 East 5th Avenue, Cambridge, MA; (821) 342-6015, officially filed as a Massachusetts corporation on June 3, 1982, and received its approval from the State of Massachusetts with stock on August 10, 1983.

The purpose of the new corporation was to import and market, in the United States and its environs, the Loose Glove line of products.

B. PRINCIPAL PRODUCTS

The Loose Glove collection includes very loose, medium loose, not-so-loose and custom-made gloves.

C. ACTIVITIES TO DATE

1. Established twenty-eight (28) person sales force in 11 territories nationally, using top quality manufacturers' agents who sell on commission within an assigned territory.

2. Attended four (4) major national trade shows.

3. Started major trade advertising program under the heading **"Loosen up for less."**

   Major Commitments from:

   a. Maxwell's—Three (3) Regions, 300 plus stores.

   b. C.J. Nickel—Western Region.

   c. Droopingdale's—East Coast, 85 stores.

   d. Melvin's—West Coast, 95 stores.

   e. Other small department stores.

5. Over six hundred (600) inquiries from recent trade advertising.

6. Contracting for major consumer advertising in major publications.

D. UNREALIZED POTENTIAL OF LOOSE GLOVES LTD.

1. Product line is unique in its design, cosmetically attractive, and priced well under the market with a forty-five percent (45%) margin on the average selling price of all products.

   In today's market, a quality brand name of gloves is priced to retail from forty dollars ($40.00) to over fifty dollars ($50.00). Most of these costs are heavy marketing expenses, endorsements, etc.

   Loose can "LOOSEN UP FOR LESS," providing TOP QUALITY GLOVES, Cosmetically Attractive for at least ten dollars ($10.00) under the market. In some cases, we can profitably provide the consumer with a twenty-five dollar ($25.00) to thirty dollar ($30.00) savings on the same quality goods with a very healthy margin for both the retailer and **Loose Gloves Ltd.**

2. The name **Loose** is timely because of the new craze for staying loose.

3. The retailer loves the volume of the industry, but not the margin, with Loose you can **"Loosen up for Less."**

4. Expansion of product line can occur into Loose apparel as well as other accessory products with our name and logo such as: Loose Socks, Handbags, Underwear, etc.

    Loose Gloves Ltd. has already been contacted by three major mills to develop a joint venture apparel company to use our new brand!

E. REQUIRED FINANCING

Loose Gloves Ltd. has a multi-staged recommendation for funding that would prove profitable and exciting for venture capitalists.

1. $300,000—Immediate requirement to solidify, the first year's sales forecast.
2. $1,000,000 Venture Capital Funding* is desired for stock interest in the corporation. This investment is for proper achievement of the Five-Year Plan, i.e., $15,000,000 in Sales.

*Naturally much more of the funding for this venture would be placed in the best available market funds, T-Bills, etc., to provide maximum profit and leverage with our banking arrangements.

F. PLANNED ALLOCATION OF FUNDS

1. VENTURE-CAPITAL $1,000,000
    a. Letter of credit investment in cost of goods. Because of our remarkable letter of credit cost of goods, this investment has minimal risk for the company—gloves is a growth industry where there is always a resaleable price for inventory of gloves at some price that is above our cost of goods, even with overstock. Terms of letter of credit are sight, plus 60 days.
    b. Warehousing fixtures and new investment location (already selected) could handle $15 million in sales and provide expandable profits for **Loose Gloves Ltd.** with a real estate investment.

   c. National Advertising Budget

   (1.) Hands Illustrated.

   (2.) Handle's Bizarre.

   (3.) Finger's Publication.

   d. Trade Advertising (see Budget).

   e. Co-op Advertising program with key accounts.

   f. Additional Employees

   (1.) Vice President of Finance and Controller.

   (2.) Warehouse and Traffic Manager.

   (3.) Telemarketing and Customer Service Department.

   (4.) Office Equipment: Word Processor and Personal Computer.

SECTION III   THE MARKETING PLAN

A. MARKETING STRATEGIES—"LOOSEN UP FOR LESS"

The Glove Industry has the following problems and opportunities for the retailer:

1. High Volume—gloves is the biggest single category in the apparel business representing a minimum of thirty percent (30%) of all sales in a full-line store and eighty percent (80%) in specialty stores like "Loose Lips."

2. Retail selling prices of all leather and split leather gloves are increasing. Example: All gloves are retailing for $40.00 to $55.00 and even higher. However the F.O.B. Orient for these gloves is approximately $10.00.

3. The import manufacturers like 5 Fingers, etc., are spending five dollars ($5.00) to ten dollars ($10.00) per glove on promotion on their product. This raises cost of goods (retail).

4. The Retailer—even the major retailer averages slightly more than forty percent (40%) on their goods.

5. The retailer is unhappy with the margin, but very happy with the volume.

6. The consumer pays the premium for the goods, F.O.B Factory.

B. PRICING STRATEGIES

1. Loose can provide the consumer with a better value (price and quality) and the retailer with a much higher margin of profit.

2. In short, a New Brand Name to "LOOSEN UP FOR LESS."

3. The margin of profit of Loose is computed and based upon the necessary selling prices for the specific category of products.

C. SALES FORCE

1. Loose has split the country into twelve (12) different geographical zones with a manufacturer's representative organization assigned to each territory.

2. Current number of salespeople exceeds fifty-five (55) and the number is growing monthly.

3. A separate national account representative has been assigned to the major accounts.

4. A new special accounts Sales Manager has joined our firm to work on special projects.

   a. Premium industry with a separate sales force.

   b. Catalog showroom sales.

   c. Tie in promotion with other related companies.

   d. Licensing opportunities for the corporation.

5. A new separate sales force will be established to handle the apparel industry, dance and exercise clubs and show retailers which are a totally different channel of distribution from sporting goods and mass marketing operations.

D. TARGET ACCOUNTS

Loose is approaching all sizes of retailers in varied industries and categories as long as the accounts will not heavily undercut the pricing and discount structure of our line. Loose is already pre-discounted to **"Loosen up for Less."** We want our accounts to make more money and greater margins!

Specific Account Categories

1. Major Department Stores
2. National Variety Stores
3. Major Mass Marketing Firms
4. Department Store Chains

E. ADVERTISING AND PROMOTIONS

1. Trade Advertising—We have started a major activity in 1984 as "THE PROFIT ALTERNATIVE" that was run in three (3) major trade publications. We have received over seven hundred (700) account inquiries in the last three (3) months. We will increase our advertising in 1985.

2. Consumer Advertising is now planned as follows:
   a. Hands Illustrated.
   b. Glove World.
   c. Fingers Publication.

3. Co-op Advertising—Key Retailer
   a. We have put aside three percent (3%) for Co-op Advertising for national sales.
   b. We will allocate these funds to major accounts for maximum retailing exposure.

4. Sponsoring tournaments and sporting activities.

5. Major trade shows, the list is endless with four (4) majors.

6. New trade show exhibit for best image!

F. BRAND NAME RECOGNITION

We believe that the New Brand "Loose" has a tremendous opportunity for consumer acceptance because of the positive impression of physical fitness that is associated with Loose Gloves.

Loose Means: "Good For You"...Physical Fitness

Loose Has: A much better opportunity for success than the many new brands that have captured the heart of the consumer.

Which would you buy if you had never heard a new brand?

Tight	Our new brand name
Stiff	is much stronger than
Wells	theirs was when they
5 Fingers	started!

We think we have a great head start advantage. However, we have more than just a great new brand. We have the outstanding quality, great styling and lower pricing, better margins...
"Loosen up for Less."

G. MAJOR COMPETITORS

1. Buyers and consumers are very major brand conscious.
2. Despite the lower margins, the limited shelf space makes for a very difficult entry to the retailer.
3. Major competitors have:
   a. Resources—money.
   b. Successful track record.
   c. Brand acceptance.
   d. Good marketing.
   e. Strong sales force.
   f. Continuity in sales.
   g. Good distribution.
4. Shortcoming of Competitors
   a. Over-priced (25%).
   b. Fat and over-staffed.
   c. Unconcerned with the retailer margin.
   d. Same import factories as Loose means we have comparable products for less.
   e. Vulnerable to a well-timed, well-formulated strategy, a great new quality brand with seasoned marketing people with a game of "Loosen Up For Less."

SECTION IV—SELECTED FINANCIAL INFORMATION

LOOSE GLOVES LTD.
PROJECTED INCOME STATEMENT
FOR THE FIRST YEAR OF OPERATIONS

	Jan.	Feb.	Mar.	Apr.	May
Sales	—	90,000	125,000	150,000	225,000
Cost of Sales @ 55%		49,500	68,750	82,500	123,750
Gross profit	—	40,500	56,250	67,500	101,250
Sales commissions @ 6%		5,400	7,500	9,000	13,500
Advertising @ 3%		2,700	3,750	4,500	6,750
Trade shows	2,000	2,000	4,000	2,000	2,000
Sales material	1,000	1,000	1,000	2,000	2,000
Trade advertising	2,000	3,000	5,000	4,000	4,000
Sales salaries	2,000	2,000	2,000	3,000	3,000
Secretarial	1,500	2,000	2,000	2,000	2,000
Travel and entertainment	3,000	3,000	4,000	3,000	3,000
Executive salaries	4,000	4,000	6,000	6,000	6,000
Accounting	1,000	1,000	1,000	1,000	1,000
Legal	5,000				
Administration cost	1,000	1,000	1,000	1,000	1,500
Rent	3,000	3,000	3,000	3,000	3,000
Warehouse expense		1,500	1,500	1,500	1,500
Interest expense		500	500	500	600
Total	25,500	32,100	42,250	42,500	49,850
Pre-tax income	(25,500)	8,400	14,000	25,000	51,400
Estimated taxes		—	—	4,000	10,000
Net income	(25,500)	8,400	14,000	21,000	41,400

Jun.	Jul.	Aug.	Sep.	Oct.	Nov.	Dec.	Total
250,000	250,000	250,000	250,000	200,000	300,000	410,000	2,500,000
137,500	137,500	137,500	137,500	110,000	165,000	225,500	1,375,000
112,500	112,500	112,500	112,500	90,000	135,000	184,500	1,125,000
15,000	15,000	15,000	15,000	12,000	18,000	24,600	150,000
7,500	7,500	7,500	7,500	6,000	9,000	12,300	75,000
—	—	—	—	2,000	1,000	3,000	18,000
1,000	1,000	1,000	1,000	1,000	1,000	1,000	14,000
3,000	3,000	3,000	3,000	3,000	4,000	3,000	40,000
4,000	4,000	4,000	4,000	4,000	4,000	4,000	40,000
2,000	2,000	2,000	2,000	2,000	2,000	2,000	23,500
4,000	3,000	3,000	3,000	4,000	3,000	4,000	40,000
6,000	6,000	6,000	6,000	6,000	6,000	6,000	68,000
1,000	1,000	1,000	1,000	1,000	1,000	1,000	12,000
							5,000
1,500	1,500	2,000	2,000	2,000	2,500	2,500	19,500
3,000	3,000	3,000	3,000	3,000	3,000	3,000	36,000
1,500	1,500	1,500	1,500	1,500	2,000	2,000	17,500
600	600	700	700	700	800	800	7,000
50,100	49,100	49,700	49,700	48,200	57,300	69,200	565,500
62,400	63,400	62,800	62,800	41,800	77,700	115,300	559,500
20,000	31,700	31,400	31,400	20,900	38,850	57,650	245,900
42,400	31,700	31,400	31,400	20,900	38,850	57,650	313,600

LOOSE GLOVES LTD.
PROJECTED BALANCE SHEET
AFTER ONE YEAR OF OPERATION

ASSETS

Cash	$ 668,200
Accounts receivable	710,000
Inventory	500,500
TOTAL ASSETS	$ 1,878,700

LIABILITIES AND STOCKHOLDERS' EQUITY

LIABILITIES

Accounts payable	$ 69,200	
Income tax payable	245,900	
TOTAL LIABILITIES		$ 315,100

STOCKHOLDERS' EQUITY

Capital Stock	1,300,000	
Retained earnings	263,600	1,563,600
TOTAL LIABILITIES AND STOCKHOLDERS' EQUITY		$ 1,878,700

LOOSE GLOVES LTD.
PROJECTED STATEMENT OF CHANGES IN CASH
FOR THE FIRST YEAR OF OPERATIONS

CASH USED FOR OPERATIONS:	
Net income	$ 313,600
Add income taxes payable	245,900
Increase in accounts payable	69,200
Increase in inventory	(710,000)
Increase in accounts receivable	(500,500)
TOTAL CASH USED BY OPERATIONS	(581,800)
OTHER USES OF CASH	
Payment of existing debt	50,000
TOTAL USES OF CASH	(631,800)
CASH PROVIDED	
By the issuance of stock	1,300,000
INCREASE IN CASH FOR THE PERIOD	668,200
CASH IN THE BEGINNING OF THE PERIOD	—
CASH AT THE END OF THE PERIOD	$ 668,200

SECTION V—THE MANAGEMENT TEAM

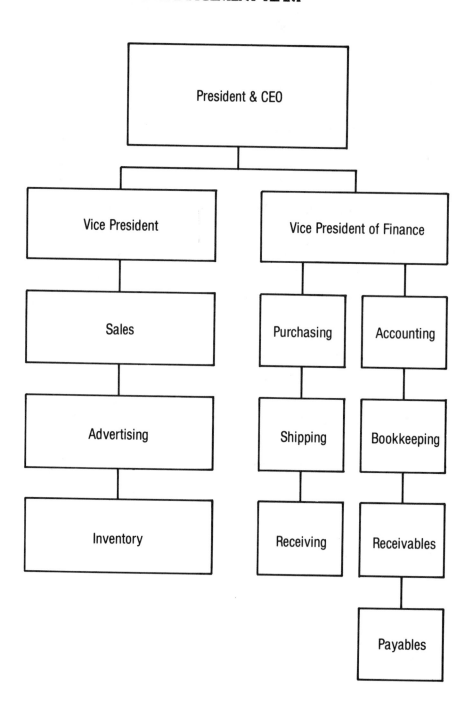

COMPANY'S MANAGEMENT TEAM

The following short biographical sketches describe the company's management:

BILL W. SMITH—PRESIDENT and CEO

Age 40, married, resides in Cambridge, Massachusetts. Developer and founder of Loose Gloves Ltd. Completed Electrical Technology and Electrical Engineering Degrees in the Army. Attended the University of California and the University of Ohio in the evenings for Business Management study.

ACME EQUIPMENT COMPANY, Akron, Ohio
Sales manager

Reported to president. Customers were primarily Blue Chip Companies in a five county area. Was one of the top salesmen for all but the first of five years with the company.

REGENCY METALS, Los Angeles, CA
General Sales Manager

Reported to and worked closely with the vice president and president. Responsible for *Profit* and *Loss,* estimating, engineering, quality assurance production training, production improvement programs and organization, advertising, Government Administrator, as well as establishing a distributor sales network.

Instituted better purchasing procedures, introduced inventory control, implemented production training programs and certifications while introducing a quality assurance program to increase productivity.

Established efficient estimating procedures, costing and coordinated with engineering, purchasing, and management for profit and loss.

Worked with vice president on all advertising materials including magazine articles and buying advertising space.

Instituted a distribution network for the company and increased the sales volume from $300,00 maximum per year to over $5,000,000 in five years.

J.C. CORNFRIED—Vice President of Marketing

Age 37, married, resides in Cambridge, Massachusetts

MBA Degree—California State University, Los Angeles

WILKINSON COMPANY, Akron, Ohio
Sales Manager

Responsible for *Profit* and *Loss* on all projects. Worked on a percentage of the profits and/or losses for commissions. Reported to and worked closely with the manager, vice president and president of the company.

During the last two years, was responsible for 45% of sales in a four-man sales staff.

Estimation, design, sales, engineering, purchasing, job cost, shop follow, installation and service were each salesman's responsibility.

— Improved purchasing procedures.

— Increased shop productivity by as much as 25% and 15% with the introduction of separate production procedures.

— Increased utilization of manufacturing floor space, preventing necessity to increase shop by 50% during a critical time when sales were at two times the annual sales of any previous year.

GEORGE E. SANDERS—Vice President of Finance

Age 48, married, resides in Cambridge, Massachusetts

B.S.M.E. Degree—Massachusetts State University
Registered Professional Engineer—Ohio and Pennsylvania

THE HARLEY COMPANY, Boston, Massachusetts

Joined the company in 1965 and has been the Vice President of Finance since 1974. Directs and supervises all administrative and financial functions of the firm.

PERSONNEL HIRING PRACTICES

As funds become available and production starts, additional personnel will be hired. The company personnel philosophy includes:

— Always hire the best qualified individual available.

— Always look for someone who can take your position.

— Always hire someone who is smarter than you are as it will make your job easier.

— Always look for a self-starter who requires little motivation.

— Always seek out the "doer."

— Always check and try to locate someone that will be comfortable, compatible and blend into our work force.

—Always encourage employees to be free thinkers and be open to constructive comments.

— NEVER HIRE A "YES" MAN.

SECTION VI—FACTORS TO CONSIDER

A. The company has limited operations to date.

B. The strength of competitors makes it a difficult industry to enter.

C. The company is dependent on key individuals.

D. The company is in debt in the amount of $50,000. Therefore, first monies raised will be used to retire company debt.

SECTION VII—PROJECTIONS, A LOOK AT THE COMPANY'S FUTURE

LOOSE GLOVES LTD.
PROJECTED INCOME STATEMENT
FOR THE FIRST FIVE YEARS OF OPERATIONS

	Year 1	Year 2
SALES	$ 2,500,000	$ 5,500,000
COST OF GOODS SOLD	1,375,000	3,025,000
GROSS PROFIT	1,125,000	2,475,000
EXPENSES	565,500	1,320,000
PRE-TAX INCOME	559,500	1,155,000
ESTIMATED TAXES	245,900	577,500
NET INCOME	$ 313,600	$ 577,500

Year 3	Year 4	Year 5
$ 8,500,000	$ 11,000,000	$ 15,000,000
4,675,000	6,050,000	8,250,000
3,825,000	4,950,000	6,750,000
2,125,000	2,750,000	3,500,000
1,700,000	2,200,000	3,250,000
850,000	1,100,000	1,625,000
$ 850,000	$ 1,100,000	$ 1,625,000

LOOSE GLOVES LTD.
PROJECTED BALANCE SHEET
AFTER FIVE YEARS OF OPERATION

ASSETS

Cash	$ 191,100
Accounts receivable	3,125,000
Inventory	2,000,000
Building—warehouse	1,500,000
TOTAL ASSETS	$ 6,816,100

LIABILITIES AND STOCKHOLDERS' EQUITY

LIABILITIES		
Accounts payable	$ 300,000	
Mortgage payable	800,000	
TOTAL LIABILITIES		$ 1,100,000
STOCKHOLDERS' EQUITY		
Capital stock	1,300,000	
Retained earnings	4,416,100	5,716,100
TOTAL LIABILITIES AND STOCKHOLDERS' EQUITY		$ 6,816,100

LOOSE GLOVES LTD.
PROJECTED STATEMENT OF CHANGES IN CASH
FOR THE FIRST FIVE YEARS OF OPERATIONS

CASH USED FOR OPERATIONS:

Net income		$ 4,466,100
Increase in accounts payable		300,000
Increase in inventory		(2,000,000)
Increase in accounts receivable		(3,125,000)
TOTAL CASH USED BY OPERATIONS		(358,900)

OTHER USES OF CASH

Payment of existing debt	$ 50,000	
Payment of warehouse	1,500,000	1,550,000
TOTAL USES OF CASH		(1,908,900)

CASH PROVIDED

By the issuance of stock	1,300,000	
Mortgage on building	800,000	2,100,000
INCREASE IN CASH FOR THE PERIOD		191,100

CASH IN THE BEGINNING OF THE PERIOD		—
CASH ON HAND AT THE END OF THE PERIOD		$ 191,100

Index

INDEX